Caring

Caring

Tarthang Tulku

Dharma Publishing

Caring is the first in a new series of books
by Tarthang Tulku

ISBN 978-0-89800-119-8
Library of Congress Control Number: 2018949545

Copyright © 2018 Dharma Publishing

Printed in the USA by Dharma Mangalam Press,
Ratna Ling, 35755 Hauser Bridge Road,
Cazadero, CA 95421

10   9   8   7   6   5   4   3   2   1

Contents

Preface

The material contained in this book had its origins in a series of conversations with several different editors over a number of months. The editors took notes and wrote them up, and we engaged in several rounds of feedback that led to substantial revisions. For the most part the conversations were held separately, and the editors did not collaborate with one another until later in the process. As a result, different sections may have somewhat different tones, and some of the same topics are revisited from different angles.

This was a deliberate decision on my part, for I wanted to find several different ways of making the same fundamental points. We have all walked different roads; we all respond to different things. Caring is of such great importance to all our lives, that it seemed to me crucial to provide as many pathways in to an exploration of caring as possible.

My request to the editors was that they express my thoughts in simple and accessible language. I was speaking out of my experience and reflections, and I did not want the material to sound too theoretical or abstract. Each of us goes through a journey in the course of our lives, and my intention was to share some of what I had learned on my own journey, so that readers could put it to use in their journeys.

I have lived in America for fifty years. During that time, I have overseen the creation of a mandala of organizations, as well as a physical mandala of temples and gardens that symbolizes in a tangible way the possibility for Tibetan Buddhism to have an impact on this culture. I have created art, made financial decisions, and had countless conversations with Americans in all walks of life and many disciplines. I have continued to write books, and I have dedicated whatever resources I could to the preservation of the heritage of the Tibetan Buddhist tradition that I love and cherish.

In all these activities, I have relied less on my Buddhist training and more on my interactions with Americans and other Westerners. After so many years of daily meetings and planning sessions, I have almost forgotten how to speak conversational Tibetan. It has been an on-the-job training, and I am deeply grateful to the West, to my students and friends, and to the guarantee of freedom of religion that helps make America the great country that it is.

The fundamental American guarantee of freedom of religion has made all this possible. Together, our community has accomplished something substantial. For my part, I am satisfied that I have not wasted people's time and energy.

What I have learned above all is the importance of care. If I had not cared about preserving the Dharma, my work would never have come to fruition. Care makes all good things happen: that is the message I wish to share.

Care is not a difficult topic to understand, and it is not even difficult to put into practice. Everyone knows how to care for themselves, their loved ones, and their community. But what we know in principle we do not always embody ourselves. We can use all the right language, say all the right words, without really committing ourselves to caring fully and deeply.

What I say here is not new. In some ways, you know it already. Still, I urge you to take these ideas seriously. Whatever you believe to have value will not be of much benefit if you do not manifest your convictions through cultivating care and putting it into practice. However, if you do care, you will achieve tangible results. You will learn to trust yourself, and this will let others trust you as well. Then you will be able to march forward together, leaving footprints for future generations to find, and perhaps to follow.

If these thoughts help you awaken to the importance of care, they may prove to be of some use, both for you and for those with whom you come in contact. Eventually, they may have a positive impact on this culture and these times.

I would like to acknowledge the work of many hands in the production of this book. My editors—Abbe Blum, Hugh Joswick, Jack Petranker, and Julia Witwer —prepared and organized the manuscript. Barbara Belew helpfully provided the introduction and the final section of the book. My middle and youngest daughters, Pema Gellek and Tsering Gellek, both reviewed the material, and made valuable contributions. Robin Caton, with great kindness and on very short notice, proofread and copyedited the work. Sally Sorenson and Ron Spohn, working to my directions with remarkable speed, designed and formatted this book; Ralph McFall and the patient, hardworking staff of Dharma Mangalam Press saw it printed and bound. To them all I extend my deep gratitude.

Caring is my offering to all who are in need of care— but in particular to those dedicated Westerners with whom I have worked for all these years. To the friends, students, supporters and volunteers who have made my projects possible, I offer you this book with my thanks. I hope you will find something meaningful and beneficial within its pages.

Tarthang Tulku
Odiyan, June 2018

Introduction

If you are reading this book, you have been given the precious gift of a human existence. You are one of billions of human beings currently covering the earth. As humans, we busily live our lives and do not always recognize our need for each other. We make our way through each day, responding as best we can to life's demands. Yet at some point we realize that all our hard work has not led to satisfaction or happiness.

We look back and wonder where the time went. We look forward and realize that our time remaining in this life is unknown. The days that we have left, whether they are few or many, are very precious. But what can we do to use the time we have today that will lead to a different result?

We are caught up in a remarkable moment in history, a moment when technology promises and delivers an amazing amount of 'improvement.' The ongoing rapid creation of ever 'better' products pulls us to want, and to believe we need, the next new thing. What we own becomes increasingly important as we strive to gain and maintain status and the security we believe status promises. The image we present to others, too, takes on increasing importance.

Through great effort we are able to present to the world the external evidence that we are successful, and that all is well with us. But internally we know that this wonderful façade is just that—a construction that must be maintained at all cost to cover what is missing from our lives: happiness and a sense of satisfaction.

Behind the façade, we live with doubts about our own value, fears of being found wanting, and guilt over choices we have made. We do not believe we are worthy of the love and respect of others, and compliments slide off the façade because we believe they are based only on what we wish others to see. We cannot imagine that they could see goodness in us if we allowed them inside our carefully constructed exterior.

Negative thoughts and worries lead to depression and anxiety. Exaggerated fantasies of what our life could and should be take hold, prompting us to do more and more of what we think will bring satisfaction, or at least reduce our pain and fear. We put pressure on ourselves to make it all better, but we are so caught up in our usual solutions we don't recognize that more of the same is not the answer. And each day just brings more frustration and fear.

We have lost ourselves in trying to find personal satisfaction, and in the process, we have lost sight of everything else. In the process, we may be losing our ability to care. We are bombarded with news of tragedy from every part of our world, and we see evidence of suffering in our own communities, but we cannot look for very long at those who are suffering; up close, and lived as a daily reality, their pain is overwhelming.

Confronted with suffering wherever we turn, we grow numb. What can one person ever do that would alleviate any small part of the problems that lead to such terrible tragedy and pain in our homes, our communities and the world? How could one person make a real difference? We resort to 'hoping' things will get better, although there is no evidence that lack of action will bring positive change.

Our focus on the appearance of things keeps us from looking within, and from seeing that each action or lack of action has consequences. The words we speak, the ways we interact, our gestures, our thoughts and the ways we express them all affect those around us. Our unwillingness or inability to interact also sends a message, often received as evidence that we do not care. And the truth is that while we may want to see ourselves as caring, it is too frightening to open our hearts when we don't believe we could offer anything that would make a difference.

It takes effort to pay attention to our own actions. It takes time to stop and reflect on the impact of what we say and do. To put in the effort and take the time would require us to care about others and about ourselves in an almost revolutionary way; and it would have to matter enough that we would do the hard work of making changes.

We might find ourselves wondering if it really even is worth it to try something different, or if making changes in how we live our lives could ever lead to something better. We are familiar with our current path, and we think we can continue doing what we have always done in our attempts to avoid (or at least cover up) the suffering that takes up so much of our energy. It can be very frightening to try a new path with an unclear destination. It is so much easier and much more predictable to stay with what we know, no matter the costs.

Where would we even start? If we reallocate any small part of the energy that goes into maintaining our protective façade, would it all crumble and leave us exposed? What would our friends and family, and others, think of us then? What if we and they learned things about us that we believe are better left hidden and unexplored? What if they discovered how little we care for ourselves?

So the dilemma grows, in large part because we are so focused on our own suffering that we cannot see beyond it. Yet if we are all caught in similar dilemmas, there are significant repercussions that each of us—in our families, communities, states and nations—live with every day.

We are losing ourselves—our humanity, our souls, our compassion, our awareness, our very lives—to the suffering we allow to control us, and dictate where and how we focus our energy.

In our zeal to maintain the façade, we mistake our efforts as evidence that we are caring for ourselves. In fact, we are not caring for anything but the façade, which is not who we are. It is only a construction that hides us from our own true selves. Our fears tell us it is better to maintain this cover because our true selves would not measure up to the standard we have set for an acceptable presentation to others.

It is clear that there are real consequences to continuing on our current path, and that those consequences affect us in real ways every day. We are left with no energy to care about the ways that our individual suffering and our attempts to alleviate it are affecting us all.

Because so many of us are on the same destructive path, we are losing the teachings and wisdom that remind us where happiness, joy, and satisfaction are to be found.

As a result, we are losing contact with the important knowledge that our senses provide us in abundance throughout each day. We do not understand how our minds work, and that our thoughts do not represent truths, but rather serve to perpetuate the ongoing narrative that maintains the façade we cling to so desperately. We have lost awareness of the valuable wisdom our emotions could provide, choosing to view feelings as something to suppress because they are unpredictable, and therefore frightening.

And so we do not take care of such important things as which thoughts we attend to, the feelings that arise throughout the day, what our senses bring us, or how we communicate with others. This means we have chosen not to contact the very parts of our being that can help us find satisfaction and a sense of well-being. We have made the error of assuming that our thoughts are sufficient to get us out of the mess in which we find ourselves, even though our thoughts have played a large role in creating that mess.

This also means we have lost the ability to care about the gifts we have been given, which could move us toward enlightenment: our hearts, minds, souls, emotions and senses. We have even lost the compass that could help us evaluate the effects of our choices, words, thoughts and actions, leaving us without a stable point of reference for the guidance we need in our struggles.

If we should decide we want something different for the life that remains to us, what are we to do?

One step is to recognize and appreciate that we are always in this moment. There are many resources available to us if we are willing to stop accepting that what we are right now is not all we are capable of being and becoming. The admonition to 'be here now' is something we have heard, but we may not know how to go about it or understand why it matters.

When we choose to be present, we demonstrate an intention and willingness to contact all that each moment brings: the thoughts that arise, the feelings that are present, our sensory connections with the physical world, our interactions with other beings, and more.

To grow in our ability to maintain contact with the present moment is not an easy task, but it is something we can learn to do. Training in how our minds work can give us tools for understanding that what seems real and logical is often a fabrication without substance. We can also grow by learning how our emotions work, the complexities they represent and reveal, and how to allow the experiencing of feelings to teach us.

Learning to meditate or engaging in a spiritual practice can open us up to learning about our mission in this life and the journey ahead of us. Becoming attuned to all our senses—what we see, hear, touch, taste and smell—allows us access to genuine riches that in our haste we risk missing altogether, like a traveler who spends more time taking photos than having the experience of being somewhere new.

Taking any of these actions exposes the vulnerability of our hearts, senses and minds, and so it is also important to protect them as we learn how these precious resources work. We must be like good, trustworthy guardians of our thoughts, feelings and hearts; only when we can do this for ourselves will we be able to protect others in the same way.

Taking the action of sharing the positive and refusing to let the negative dominate can help us stay on the path to a life that is full and happy. Being aware of the work of others on this path, and remembering that we each influence others in powerful ways, is also important: for we have the choice to be a positive or a negative influence with every action we take.

If we choose to engage in our own lives more fully, we will find that we also engage with others at a deeper level. We will begin to recognize and value our interconnectedness, and to see that even small daily actions have broader impact than we previously believed. We will begin to enjoy the connections that develop beyond our immediate relationships, tying us more fully to our communities. In the process, we will learn how to communicate more positively, how to share, and how to truly care for and about others.

Building better communities requires these skills. We can work together to learn how to value each other, and how to develop a common understanding of what matters by tapping into the knowledge and wisdom that is in all of us. A willingness to learn from one other is essential.

Many of my students are from the United States—a country that has long represented freedom and opportunity to people around the world. As citizens of this nation, we need to take seriously the responsibilities that our freedoms demand, because the example we set—along with many other Western nations—is very powerful. As individuals who are part of the local and the global community, we can choose to participate with others in enjoying a good journey through this life. By harnessing the power of modern technology, we can connect with others both near and far for the purpose of understanding the journey we share during this life, as well as supporting each other's efforts to value the journey.

Those born in America have the freedom to make these choices and to act on them because our nation was founded on these rights. In America and democracies like it, if we wish to be a force for positive change in the world, there is nothing stopping us except our own lack of willingness to act. Choosing to engage more fully in our own lives provides the opportunity to gain what we say we want—happiness—for ourselves and for our world. Choosing not to engage means we lose that opportunity.

But wait, you may be thinking. This leap from simply trying to find relief from our individual suffering to taking on the happiness of the global community seems too large. Do we really want to accept that our actions have that much of an impact on anything other than our daily well-being? Wouldn't it be better to stay with the familiar struggles even though they are exhausting, and our attempts to resolve them leave us unsatisfied? At least our familiar routines can provide temporary relief, sometimes.

It is true that choosing to try something new is difficult. But it is also true that taking the risk can lead to the satisfaction and happiness we do wish to enjoy in what remains of our time in this life. Even small actions can have a bigger impact than we realize. Any opening up to the possibility of caring reverberates through all of us.

Caring, forgiveness and respect are qualities we can actively choose to develop; they will prove most valuable in our quest for positive change. These qualities are demonstrated through gestures, and embodied in words and the details of our daily interactions. Each is an important element in how we relate to ourselves, as well as in how we relate to other beings and our surroundings. The practice of each can be enhanced by our willingness to cultivate a receptive mind and to make good use of what we learn.

Caring means we treasure ourselves and others; it means we hold all life as a precious gift. When we care, we display kindness and concern; we pay attention; we nurture and protect; we are benevolent and thoughtful, considering and protecting what we treasure. Our words and actions convey the depth of our caring, because we move away from the easy ignorance of our own and others' pain to take action.

The demonstration of caring takes many forms, and is experienced by each of us in our own way. We may not always know what we need in order to feel cared for and cared about, but we know when it is not present. This is true for others as well.

We may think of caring for ourselves as a selfish act, assuming that any care we extend ourselves takes away from the caring we can offer others. But this is not true. Rather, a willingness to care for ourselves expands our ability to care for others because our hearts are open to the warmth of what is precious in each of us. We grow in our ability to care when we practice opening our hearts to all beings, including ourselves.

Forgiveness requires seeing with a broader view that allows us to let go of the need to feel we have been wronged. Forgiving allows us to release the burden of anger and hurt so that we may move forward unencumbered. It frees us for a better use of energy, and changes our interactions with those we believe have wronged us. Forgiveness does not say that what was done was right or wrong; rather, it allows us to let go of feeling the need to prove the wrongness of what has happened. We are free to live in the present, relieved of the need to blame or punish those who have caused us to suffer.

In offering pardon, we experience compassion: for those whose pain led to the actions that harmed us, and for ourselves as we carry the burden of the pain that resulted from that harm. Forgiveness offers us a respite from suffering both in the present and in the future. It is a gift we can choose to give or to withhold, but giving benefits both the giver and the receiver even when the receiver does not know it has been given.

Respect is another crucial expression of care. When we feel respect, we recognize merit. We esteem what and whom we respect, and we find ways to demonstrate our awareness of their value. We appreciate their goodness and we honor their being. We may even wish to learn from them, to develop the qualities they represent. Our admiration of what or whom we respect is based on an acceptance of all that they are, with awareness of their imperfections.

Self-respect is an equally important quality to develop. We, too, have admirable qualities in addition to our imperfections. We, too, have goodness and wisdom. Recognition of our own merit is an important step to take, because it allows us to more fully recognize the merit in others. If we are unable to respect ourselves, we will find it very difficult to extend respect to others, because we will not know how to recognize what is worthy of respect.

In this Introduction, I have reflected on how our individual need for care may lead us to consider the broader reasons why caring is important for each of us, and for the larger communities in which we live and exist. This bigger picture is important, if we wish to understand why the study of caring matters.

When we seek to alleviate our own suffering, we never act in a vacuum. We are changed, and in the process, everything is changed: how we relate to ourselves and others, how these others relate to their own lives and to themselves, and so on, as the ripples caused by our actions move outward. Depending on our awareness and understanding, the impact of what we do can create more suffering—or it can make a meaningful, tangible, beneficial difference for us all.

We can choose to be a part of the movement toward more caring and positive relationships with those in our immediate sphere, and by extension with those in the broader community of our world.

For such a small word, 'caring' carries a big wallop. When we open ourselves up to a more expansive kind of caring, we are doing something that matters for all of us. Making this commitment may require that we change in important ways, and the decision to make a change can be scary. But in choosing to care, we discover our courage. Our fears can only stop us if we let them.

I hope that what you find here will give you the encouragement you need to choose caring, to study it deeply, and express it in all that you do.

Hidden Healer

Caring is Key

When I first arrived in the United States, I did not have much knowledge of the Western world. The language, the culture, the system of education, the people—all of these were new to me. Coming in this way, I was a bit of an innocent: I had much I wanted to achieve, so I began working with people and undertaking projects, and just tried to do my best. Looking back, I can see that I sometimes made mistakes, for despite my good intentions, I didn't always know what I needed to know.

I am told that caring for forests and planting trees is an American ideal, something I have in common with the people of my adopted country. I love all kinds of plants and trees, and I appreciate their beautifully different colors and forms. And so I planted audaciously, bringing together trees from all over the world to take root in parks and gardens of the retreat center I named Odiyan.

Here at Odiyan I plant natives to support our ecology. I plant orchards of apple and citrus trees, plums and chestnuts and mulberries, and stands of gingko, flowering magnolia, and tall cypress. In the forty square acres of Odiyan's Inner Mandala I have planted hundreds of thousands of trees. If you include the hedges, shrubs and flowers planted here over the last thirty years, that number gets closer to one million.

But when I began, I didn't understand how deep the holes for my trees needed to be. I didn't think to protect the roots from gophers; I didn't know how to ensure the soil was good enough, how to determine the right balance of nutrients in the compost, how to provide the right ratio of sun and shade. It took time to recognize that many trees needed to be staked well or planted in the lee of the winds, which blow strongly from the ocean here.

Today, I can see more clearly what I didn't know thirty years ago about gardening and forestry. Many factors require attention and forethought. We must have knowledge of the properties of the local topsoil, weather patterns, and the growth habits of the trees, which once established may need annual pruning. Then there is the harvesting, which must be coordinated carefully by our small resident population, so our fruit doesn't go to waste.

Over the years we have learned how much water each tree, shrub, flower and plant really needs. And yet, from time to time, my students and I would forget to water, or let the irrigation lines go unmaintained. Then the trees were lost.

A sad realization! My investment had disappeared, and more importantly, these beautiful, inspiring life forms, almost like friends to me, were gone. These lessons taught me that I must work vigorously and plan carefully for the welfare of these precious lives in my charge.

Paying attention, staying aware, offering care; these are important in every endeavor, every area.

For when we take a closer look, everything we see seems to be suffering from lack of care, whether we consider the environment, the economy, our communities, business and government, families and relationships, art, culture and religion, or science and education. Without care in communication, people easily misinterpret one another, which can create pain and trouble for all concerned. Even the various kinds of meditation or 'mindfulness' instruction widely available today seem to be missing something in this regard.

It may be that we need a new introduction to caring. Our usual approach has not had much success; as a rule, just telling ourselves that we need to care—or that we need to receive care—does not seem to be working very well. These lectures and expressions of pain do not bring us the healing we need.

Buddhist philosophy holds that this world we take so seriously is an illusion, a mirage. We could decide, in light of that idea, that caring is not so important; after all, our existence is impermanent and insubstantial. But however temporary these circumstances may be, I believe we will find, if we look honestly at ourselves, that we all want to live happily.

We live within a framework of actions and reactions, causes and predictable effects. The plants in our garden may be part of a magical show of space—yet they respond when we give them water. We could even say that these dreams of ours need loving care, as they shine out in our awareness, growing up and showing up according to the specific patterns of this mysterious illusion-realm.

Ultimately, we are sentient beings. We want to preserve what is good, to enjoy and maintain what is precious in our lives.

Caring is the key.

Caring for Caring

What kind of care do we give to caring?

Perhaps we care a lot, about a lot of things; or maybe we say, "I have lots of worries and cares." In this case we carry our cares, a heavy burden. Maybe, instead, we are careful—watching out all day long.

When we care, we pay attention; but do we pay much attention to caring?

Most of the time, we have one method, one approach to caring. Our main method could be described as the 'of' method: we take care *of* things, of our loved ones, of ourselves. This seems not only beneficial on the face of it, but simply necessary. Plants need water; dogs need walks; children need support and attention. Our jobs must be taken care of. Our health must be looked after. When it comes to caring, what more needs to be said?

But this 'taking care of' does not necessarily convey the essence, the heart of caring. For one thing, it obeys a strictly enforced distinction between here and there, this and that, you and me.

In that respect, caring *for*, taking care *of*, and caring *about* are behaviors that are marked by mind's belief in its distance and difference from the world; they all bear traces of that painful regime.

This may be why we often experience caring—our own, and others'—as something negative: caring is what is missing from our lives, and we know it primarily through its absence.

It is as if we believe that caring is a rare medicine we cannot make anymore, something we give out, grudgingly and sparingly, until it is gone. We are left feeling drained, if we are the ones giving care; or needy and unfulfilled if we are the recipients of such care.

Nevertheless, the magic of caring is real. We may have no idea what makes it possible. But we can feel it when it's not there—and we respond joyfully when it is.

It may be hard even to imagine an alternative way of caring. But real caring may be already present, implicit in experience, waiting to be discovered and refined.

The Real Thing

We need food to live, and we can survive on food even if it has no flavor. But there are people who have mastered the art of cooking: some of us know how to make even a simple salad or a glass of fruit juice a special, memorable experience. This kind of food uplifts the spirits and nourishes heart and mind as well as body.

Real caring is like that. It has a distinctive flavor. It is a healing essence that can be distilled from experience, in much the same way that skillful cooking can bring out wonderful flavors in our food.

This special quality is caring's seal of authenticity. It is the watershed that nourishes life. We can sense its presence in thoughts and gestures, but it doesn't stop there; it runs underneath all our expressions of kindness, and is deeper and broader than any word or action.

We know caring is real when we encounter this encouraging atmosphere, this delicious flavor, this indefinable feeling of peace: we respond to it the way plants respond to moisture. This wonderful quality expresses a kind of pure caring, beyond the 'from' and 'to' of relationships, comparisons and measures.

I believe there is more to discover about caring than what we commonly understand. It may be that we can learn a new art of caring by taking a closer look, not just at *what* we care about, but at *how* we care.

Caring could permeate all we do. It could shine through in every facet of our work. It could reveal beauty at the heart of our most basic activities. Eating, sleeping, talking with friends, washing dishes—when our ordinary lives are invested with the quality of caring, they are transformed.

Learning how to care might mean learning to care not only for one or two things—our favorite things, or the things that worry us the most. We could learn to open our hearts to this quality of expansive, unconditional caring, experiencing and expressing it for ourselves.

Expressions of Caring

When it is truly alive in us, caring is more than a theory. It comes out in how we live our ordinary lives— how we do our jobs, support our family members, and relate to our community and environment.

It's important that caring come out in perceptible, practical, real-life ways. Keeping spaces clean, cooking healthy and delicious food, or showing others a gentle attitude and calm temper can sometimes express our caring far more effectively than flowery words.

For as we know from our own experience, sometimes words cannot go deep enough to change anything inside us. We need to find a way to convey real caring to ourselves and others that gets down inside our hearts and minds, where the soil is fertile, and seeds of new possibilities can grow.

In this field of active caring, our actions communicate as well as our words.

Behavior like this can be quickly recognized, appreciated, and emulated by others—no special instructions or insight required. It shines out in the way we treat our tools, the way we cook our meals, the way our houses and gardens feel to be in. It shows in how we move down the street, how we engage our duties as citizens or members of the community. Real caring is immediately apparent in how we clean up after ourselves, how we maintain and repair and strengthen what is weak.

Caring doesn't leave the hard work to others, or imagine that some abstract body—'they'—will fix everything and pay for everything. When we really care, we take care of it ourselves, quickly and without any fuss.

When we really embody this caring knowledge, we say, "No problem: consider it done."

Real caring shows up in real respect for others; it takes time to appreciate their efforts and encourage their growth and development. If someone does something nice—for you, for their family, for the community—caring takes notice. In this way, caring inspires caring.

Caring Includes You

We can easily understand how important it is to feel appreciated, when we see how helpful and beneficial appreciation is to the people around us. And yet we rarely appreciate ourselves.

We don't normally take the time to celebrate small victories and achievements, or to encourage ourselves when we practice caring. Be honest: how often have you told yourself, "Well done! This was worth the time and effort. That self of mine did a good job—let's rejoice!"

Some of us never hear these words from ourselves.

Yet this self-encouragement and self-support lend us the strength to accomplish much, to improve. As we improve, we gain self-respect; in time, self-respect becomes self-confidence. We can feel an honest self-appreciation that lets us recognize our own virtues.

After all, you noticed the need, you offered kindness and care. Your discipline, sincerity, and kindness brought some good into the world. That goodness is eminently worthy of notice.

Does it seem selfish to say so? We might think so at first, for as a rule we are little used to the idea that deep appreciation, even for ourselves, is an essential part of caring.

We can see very clearly the benefits of caring; we can see just as clearly the consequences when care is lacking. We can take a little time to examine our own lives, and see the same patterns play out in human history: at every scale, in every situation, we can see the difference caring makes.

Caring brings out the best in us. It supports big, ambitious projects, and gives depth and meaning to our knowledge. But caring doesn't only manifest in big gestures: it's also there in the tiny details. Even just paying attention, staying calm, and weighing what we say before we speak can contribute to an atmosphere of real caring. This is caring all of us can do.

And caring is magnetic, attractive: it inspires others to care, too.

How to Work with This Book

Woven into this book, you will find some unusual additions.

Expressions, shown in italics, pour out the heart's feelings—its longings, fears, and discoveries. You may not feel all the things these expressions share, but perhaps you can empathize with some of them.

Exercises offer points to explore practically for yourself. Depending on the exercise, you might engage these points through your body and senses, your thoughts and memories, or the spirit of your imagination.

Explorations contain suggestions for developing some of the practical skills of caring, as well as reflections on real-life situations many of us face.

If you like this book, I recommend that you try reading it three times, or in three ways: once looking deeply into your experience to see if you can discover the essence of caring; a second time concentrating on the inner healing that caring makes possible; and a third time exploring the way our conduct and behavior can be transformed when we open up to caring.

Hidden Elixir

This secret joy, flowing beneath and within our experience, this secret kindness! If we could really touch it—if we only knew how—if we could experience it for ourselves, then we would have a great inner resource, the foundation of well-being, strength and happiness. We would have an unshakable sense of our own value, and a pathway to a deeply meaningful life.

My father, Sogpo Tulku, was not only a lama, a counselor, and a community leader; he was also a fully-trained Tibetan physician. When I was a child, assisting him as he cared for the people in our valley, he told me of special healing herbs that grew in the mountains.

The knowledge of these healing herbs was transmitted in a special way. Teachers did not tell their students how to harvest the plants. The texts explained the uses and virtues of the plants, but did not describe what they looked like, or where they were to be found. To find the herbs, it was necessary to study the teacher's movements carefully—for it was his footprints alone that could lead the student to the right plant.

Perhaps the inner elixir of caring is similar. Advisors, teachers and texts can tell you what the medicine does, but not how to find it for yourself.

I hope these words will serve as pointers, the way my father's footsteps revealed the secret location of precious medicines that help and heal.

Caring for Origins

Understanding some of the basic features of our existence as sentient beings can help us identify the importance of caring.

Before We Begin

Why should we care for our origins? Does it matter where we came from—or make a difference to what we experience here and now, today?

It may prove more important than we realize.

For woven deep into our being are conditions with very ancient causes—conditions that cause us, in turn, to behave in ways that continue to harm us, individually and collectively.

If we want to experience, understand and offer caring in a new way, we must be sure that the water reaches down to the roots; if we want to make more than a superficial difference, we must understand as deeply as we can what has pressed us into the positions we occupy today.

As you read, continue to ask yourself: *Where do I come from? What contributed to my being this person, in this way, in this place and time? What have I got invested in this—where are my time and energy going within this set-up?*

Is this way of being inevitable?

Right Here, Right Now

Here we are: right here, right now, in this time and place. To signal this, we say that we are present, or that we inhabit the present moment. Everybody knows this is so; everybody agrees. There is nothing controversial here, nothing to inquire into.

Still, we can ask what we really mean when we say, "I am present."

First, the act of locating the self seems to require that we also *present* the self. For this to be possible, we have to make some additional claims. For instance, I seem to be saying that my present presence is a by-product of a temporal structure that separates the past and future from the present. Also, being here means that I *could* be elsewhere—otherwise, the statement would be meaningless.

Not only that, but for me to be present, I must have an
identity that sets me apart from other things or entities. I am here, and other things are there.

Behind all this, there is a structure in place that presupposes the possibility of movement. I am here because I am not there. How did I get here? There must
have been a transition, a going. I was there, and now,
through some kind of movement, I have gone 'from'
there 'to' here. The possibility is always open that the
movement will continue: that I will go from this present 'here' to another 'there' (which will, of course, then
become my new 'here').

At this point, we have seen enough to recognize that
being here depends on a whole set of structures in space
and time. I have arrived here from somewhere else;
'from' that starting place, I have come to here. How
did that structure—from and to, here and there—get
set up?

If we take this question seriously, not just on a theoretical level but in terms of my actual present existence, I
see that I, just like you, am the product of many forces
or structures that came before me, all of them located
in what we usually call the past.

Being here, being present, I have roots—we could call
it a lineage, a 'parenthood,' or ancestry.

Where We Are From

Where we say we come from, and what we assume are our origins, tend to shift over time.

Western four-year-olds, not yet civilized, ask, "How was I made?" "Where do I come from?" "What is God?" "Why do people die," and "why can't I stay up late?" These basic questions make adults uncomfortable. "That's the way it is," "Because," "I don't know" or "Go to sleep" are familiar responses from the stumped or exasperated.

For most of us, the circumstances of our own adult lives have forced us to abandon these lines of questioning ourselves. We may even, in moments of frustration or exhaustion, declare the questions foolish. But at what cost?

Early on our natural, open-ended curiosity takes strong hits. Exploration gets discouraged subtly and overtly. But are all the roads really closed? How might awakening into the living aspect of "where do we come from" open up new or at least deeper fields of knowledge?

At the same young age, as we learned to give up on these questions, we were being steadily woven into stories of belonging, exclusion, and identity. We grew up habitually locating ourselves in terms of family, hometown, team, state, region, country, as well as race, ethnicity and religion.

We assumed a certain identity: we belong to this group and not to that one. And we enacted stories that we continue to cognize, recognize, accept or reject, and tell about—and to—ourselves, even today.

After apprenticing to such narratives, in typical Western fashion, many of us revise our stories as we move away from home turf, family of origin, and select our own chosen intimates. We slip into wider worlds of profession, coded behaviors and cultural expertise. During later stages of life, our stories may no longer entertain, and we may tell the highlights over and over, unaware of how the narrative habit has reduced the 'juice' of experience. Relying on feedback from complex patterns drained of vigor, we may exhaust ourselves.

If we become aware of how 'who I am' depends on circumstances of birth and culture, we might begin to ask differently: "What is the beginning of the beginning?" We might turn to science, philosophy, or religion for a more satisfactory answer to that original, innocent question of where I came from. On what do we base our lives, what kinds of knowing and fundamental grounding?

In the West, both science and religion relate to origins in certain ways. God as creator provides what we might call a 'resting point' for beginnings. "God made it so" is a final answer for certain religions; this answer can be reassuring for the faithful, but it leaves God incomprehensible for scientists.

In these stories, how the creator is related to the causal conditions that continue to produce the world remains mysterious. God's character at work is pronounced unknowable for human beings, with divine judgment forbidding certain inquiries. We are marked out as non-divine, frail or sinful.

Certain views hold God as the source of infinite love and compassion, with loving others as part of the central ethic of loving God. Some philosophers of ethics may rely instead on causality as a basis for right and wrong, and see the consequences of our actions as the determining factor of our cultural norms.

These are some of the ways we have tried to answer the question of origins in our human history, but today many people find these answers as unsatisfactory as the "because" response was to the curious child.

The success of Western science in providing workable solutions to problems has given it authority in establishing what counts as knowledge in our time. Scientists follow out causes and conditions by proposing different theories based on controlled and repeatable experiments that may reach back in time to explain beginnings. Although science pursues what is testable and coherent, when it comes to the question of beginnings, it is inherently speculative and unknowable—as the many competing theories of cosmology demonstrate. Explanations cycle between what has been proven and what is regarded as *beyond knowing*—at least for now.

The explanation most people accept today as central to our human story is that we inhabit Earth, a planet within the universe. The current Western scientific narrative is that our universe began with a Big Bang around 13.7 billion years ago—with space and time emerging together from a cosmic singularity that inflated and continues to expand at a rapid pace.

Astronomers fashion maps using spacecraft satellite data to describe the oldest light in the Universe. They have deduced that the Universe is 68% dark energy, energy not understood, with dark matter that has gravity making up 27%. So according to this measured story, only 5% of the observable universe, the part we can see—including planets like our Earth, us sentient beings, the sun and galaxies, and energy such as light, heat and x-rays—is understood. The origin of these origins remains unknown.

Scientific observation has pretty much established that we live on a planet that rotates around a medium sized star we call our Sun. There are other stars within the Local Bubble, which is a region of space and dust of which our sun is a member. The closest star to the sun is approximately 4.3 light-years away in what we named the Alpha Centauri system. This Local Bubble of stars rotates around the center of our galaxy, the Milky Way. Our galaxy is home to hundreds of billions of stars. And the Milky Way itself is part of a local group of galaxies that contains the Andromeda galaxy, faintly visible to the naked eye on a still and cloudless night.

At an even grander scale, this local group is part of a great expanse of galaxies that extend in all directions, uncountable and vast, well over 200 billion galaxies in the detectable universe.

Elements In Here from Out There

Western scientists are understandably interested in our finding our place in this universe. It's said we are all made of star dust; in less poetic terms, this means that the basic elements that compose everything on earth, including our own bodies, were once formed in the heated fusion of many suns.

A recent survey of 150,000 stars revealed that humans and sentient life on this planet have about 97% of the same kinds of atoms as our Milky Way galaxy. Even the building blocks of life, the elements of carbon, hydrogen, nitrogen, oxygen, phosphorus and sulfur—the same organics found in certain meteorites—have been discovered to need starlight—ultraviolet light—in order to form as chemicals in space.

Nearly half of our bodies' elements may have formed in neighboring galaxies from giant exploding stars. Originally wafted on intergalactic winds from huge clouds of gas, the elements that make up our bodies might qualify us, according to some astrophysicists, as cosmic immigrants: for they are, in fact, visitors from other galaxies.

Unknown Roots

We may be aware of these cosmic origin-stories to a greater or lesser degree, depending on our background and interests. But this vast and inconceivable expanse does not seem to have much to do with us in any ordinary sense. How do we fit into this picture?

Looking at origins in the more familiar terms of human history, each of us can consider a wide range of specific events that brought us into being. For example, I exist as I do today because my parents gave me life and their parents gave them life, and so on, back through the generations.

On a more global level, major events took place to put me in these present circumstances: wars and opportunities for trade, migrations triggered by outbreaks of disease or fighting or famine.

We can see today how natural disasters, famines, and fighting uproot people whose ancestors may have lived in one place for centuries, and send them here and there across the face of the earth. America, the great melting pot, is perhaps a shining example of a land shaped by such upheavals, but today countries in every part of the world experience similar disruptions. It is as if a great wind periodically sweeps across the lives of millions of individuals, leaving a landscape configured in completely new ways.

In this way, countless events trace my lineage and contribute to it. Some affect many people, while others are wholly particular to me. The friends I made when I was young, a lightly-made decision to head in one direction rather than another, delaying my departure by just a few minutes at a critical moment—these are the kinds of unpredictable events that shape who I am today. Change just one of them, and I would be someone else entirely.

With effort, perhaps we can give names to all the events that these various levels of explanation single out, and we can trace, at least to some limited extent, their complex and compounded interactions. However far we take this kind of inquiry, though, it seems in the end to lead to the same outcome. What we can say with confidence is that we are the product of countless forces and events, far beyond our ability to comprehend or even identify. Every story we tell to account for the derivation of 'I am here' will be thoroughly incomplete—an almost arbitrary selection of a certain set of events and occurrences.

In turn, all such happenings unfold against a background that fades into the shadows. If we direct our gaze in some other direction, new elements and factors come into view, but when we look one way, we necessarily leave other regions in the dark.

When we consider it in that light, our real ignorance of our roots is a little daunting.

Complexity at the Limits

As a way of speaking of all these interactions, we might say that we embody countless *existents*, countless happenings. In some contexts, we could speak of fundamental particles that come together to produce what was not previously there. If we used other ways of looking, we might speak of energies, known and unknown, that flow through time, generating outcomes.

It would clearly be beyond any one person's knowledge to trace all these interactions across all possible fields of knowledge. With so many factors at work and subject to analysis, no one account of how something came to be—the parentage of what is presently so, the 'from' out of which being here emerges—can ever be complete.

The transitions that lead from past to present, from 'from' to 'to', remain at some level mysterious. We can rely on the evidence of the senses, and we are free to make use of our imagination to speculate, theorize, explain, and form hypotheses. All of that, however, will only take us so far.

Yet what other authorities can we rely on? Tradition? Reasoning from first principles? Who can give a satisfying answer to these basic questions about our origins?

Faced with these limits, science takes its own particular approach to arriving at knowledge. It looks at causality and attempts to discover links. Today it does this through extensive analysis of oceans of data, so vast that only powerful computers can sort through them, and only sophisticated statistical analysis can arrive at fruitful conclusions. Scientists in field after field combine increasingly sophisticated tools of measurement with statistical manipulation of information and algorithms that help identify links. Such methods steadily make new connections and generate new areas for research. If we are lucky, the knowledge created in this way will prove useful.

Buddhism takes its own, very different approach. It too speaks in terms of causes and conditions, but it does not mean by these only material forces acting on one another. Instead, it includes the workings of karma in the realm of causes and conditions. This brings into play 'subjective' elements that science generally chooses to exclude, for karma is grounded largely in the intention with which actions are carried out.

At first blush, scientific inquiry and Buddhist methods of examining experience seem to have little in common. Yet both scientific and Buddhist forms of inquiry share something basic—a sense of limits.

Wherever they start their investigations, the range of explanation and understanding instantly expands into the realm of the incomprehensible. Indeed, the history of modern physics seems to show that the deeper we probe into the fundamental 'particles' that make up the material world, the more their ultimate nature proves to be mysterious. Something similar could be said of the Buddhist understanding, which sees our conventional reality as true only in a relative sense, and sets ultimate reality—accessible to the vision of the enlightened ones—apart.

In confronting these challenges, science postpones possibilities for understanding to the future. We cannot presently say, for instance, how consciousness arises from matter, but most scientists will say that one day we will have the answer. In Buddhism, the 'strategy' is different: there are countless realities knowable only to those far advanced on the spiritual path, whether they exist now, in the past, or in the future.

Depths of the Mystery

For us as individuals, located here and nowhere else, unknowables operate at every level. No matter how far the range of the observable expands, certain connections remain mysterious, almost magical. At the ordinary, everyday level, we may be able to offer clear explanations and predict what is likely to happen in a given situation, but there are countless ordinary events that leave us in the dark. Why does one person recover from a vicious disease while another succumbs? How does someone of average talents rise to a position of leadership or attain success that another person, far more skilled, fails to achieve? What makes two people fall in love?

There is more. What accounts for the movement of the mind from moment to moment, without any clear connection between what appears to the mind now and what appeared a moment earlier? A long-forgotten memory bursts forth, only to give way to an unexpected image, a sudden burst of insight, or a moment of sadness. I decide to turn left instead of right, and my life is altered irreversibly by this one small decision.

How does it happen? Why should it be this way and not another? Science has its explanations, and Buddhist psychological approaches offer their own forms of analysis, but the particulars of the moment resist all such accounts.

Yet even when we cannot offer clear explanations, we cannot escape the sense that there are links between the events that make up our lives, and that those links could conceivably be traced. The microscopic and the macroscopic seem interconnected. One event depends on others, at both the outer and the inner levels. There may be those who say that events arise at random, but that is not our experience, at least not always and in every circumstance. Even when we cannot follow the thread, the parenthood of 'from' and 'to' continues to function.

It is not just that in such circumstances we suspect that there are links. The truth is that we insist on it. We may, in fact, spend our lives looking for explanations; we do our best to make sense of what has happened. If one story proves mistaken or incomplete, we turn to another.

In making sense of what arises, we can identify certain fundamentals in our experience, whatever their status may be in scientific ways of thinking. We can speak of spirit, consciousness, awareness, and cognition, or of the mind as the fundamental operator of experience.

For instance, we can speak of experience as past or present or future, even when physics has no room for such categories in its equations, for those distinctions are very much alive for us as human beings. We can identify locations in space and investigate embodiment, whether at the outer level of conventional appearance or on a more refined inner level. These are bases for what we understand to be so.

Perhaps such fundamentals can also be the vehicles of our transformation. If we could allocate these ongoing operations, going into the subtle parts of the steady stream of transitions that constitute our experience, we might learn much of value. In the mysterious, unknown depths, possibilities for understanding beckon.

Pointing at Secrets

In the Buddhist tradition, the source of deeper understanding—the understanding we need to grasp the mystery of our own origins—is wisdom. Yet wisdom itself is mysterious. When we ask what it means to see with the eye of wisdom, different answers are forthcoming. Indeed, the English word 'wisdom' is used to translate a variety of different words in Sanskrit or Tibetan, each of which transmits a range of meanings that overlaps only incompletely with other, related words.

Because this is so, confusions may arise. Ideas may be linked together that should remain separate, or distinctions may be marked out that make no sense in terms of the original vocabulary. These are difficult points, and the West is still at the very early stages of developing the understanding that would make real clarity possible. Still, we must proceed as best we can.

In Mahayana Buddhism, different schools emphasize different forms of wisdom, different ways of engaging the mysteries within which our relative truths unfold. What are known as the Second Turning teachings rely on analytic wisdom, which rests in the end on fundamental insight into *shunyata*, the term still being inadequately translated into English as 'emptiness.'

These are the teachings of the Prajnaparamita, which go beyond all conventional understanding. Since no formulation can definitively capture their inner meaning, they are presented in different forms and different texts in light of the different capacities of sentient beings.

In this way, the Buddha presented a vast array of teachings. Some have since been lost, but the depth of his realization shines through in the texts that remain.

The Mahayana teachings of the Third Turning, on the other hand, approach the ultimate mysteries differently. Here the fundamental truth of being is linked to *prabhasvara* (or *prabhasa*), a term we could translate as 'boundless radiant light,' a luminosity inseparable from knowingness and the ways that knowledgeability impresses itself on our being.

In the Third Turning teachings, shunyata leads in the direction of the co-existence of conventional appearance with the secret, inner form of being, luminous in its very nature.

Transitions such as the one from the conventional to the transcendent are said by some schools and commentaries to become available through a unique unity that instantly clarifies the mind. Like a pure and faultless crystal, or like a dynamic manifestation that inspires our thoughts and minds, this luminous way of knowing reveals the co-existence of the expressions of boundless knowledge with shunyata, the underlying openness and emptiness of all that appears.

Great Buddhist masters such as Asanga and Vasu-
bandhu have explored these interconnections in ways
that have not yet been fully investigated in the West. If
the teachings on shunyata emphasize that appearance
is empty of all substance, the teachings on prabhasa
make clear that perception has the intrinsic capacity of
knowingness.

In activating such ways of understanding, we discover
the hidden depths within our ordinary forms of perception. In our conventional understanding, we base our
knowledge and interpretations on 'from' and 'to' and on
the predetermined structures of consciousness and mind.
In this way, we form our sense of causality and connection, and we link up points to create the webs of interpretation we rely on to make sense of what we experience.

Yet in the Third Turning Sutras, the feel of our sense
faculties, the presentations of thought, and the nature
of our being are shown to be impressions and expressions of a more fundamental way of being. Clarity and
emptiness co-exist. It is this co-existence, mysterious
though it may be, that makes transformation possible.

In probing the ultimate significance of such understanding, we necessarily rely on words and language.
Using these as our tools, we do our best to project a
meaning that in the end is beyond the capacity of words
and ideas to engage. Of course, the risk is that in turning to labels and concepts, we lose meanings that are
available only on the experiential level.

It is the ancient problem of the finger pointing at the moon: the finger is not the moon, and has nothing in common with it, yet we need the finger to show us where to look. We can ask, as some Western scholars have done: Will the moon point back?

The Problem with Pointing

At another level, the problem of advancing beyond our usual knowledge to arrive at the deeper levels of wisdom can be understood as the problem of space and form. Forms arise through taking positions: for a particular form to be there, it must occupy the position that we point out as 'there'.

Yet all positioning departs from the perfect openness of space, which some Buddhist traditions identify as the source and essence of wisdom.

Space and positioning operate in different dimensions. If we speak of 'the middle of space,' our saying contradicts itself, for space as such has no edges and no boundaries. It makes no sense to speak of the middle of space, just as, when it comes to space, we cannot speak of up or down or top and bottom. In space, all directions are the same.

This is the same difficulty we have already noted. Working with words and concepts, we proceed by defining and separating. But this way of pointing out can never succeed in pointing to space itself.

This limitation has consequences for our understanding of how the senses function. For example, when we hear a sound, we automatically locate the source of the sound in terms of a mapped-out physical space. Yet for hearing as such, independent of the naming and labeling that lets us identify the source of the sound, these kinds of spatial coordinates may not make sense.

Instead of focusing on what is pointed out, perhaps it would help to look at the act of pointing.

Pointing seems to presuppose a pointer who points, and a point that is pointed out. Yet there is another way of looking at this. When we point, we cannot really separate out the act of pointing from what is pointed out. If there were no point to point at, I could not do the pointing; if I did not point, the identity of the point at which I am pointing would never emerge. One is marked out in dependence on the other. It seems we are trapped in a circle.

This circle, however, comes into being only because we rely on our concepts—on the labels that separate out pointer, what is pointed out, and the act of pointing—and then struggle to put them back together. We point things out, and in doing so, we establish their independent status, with all the problems that follow.

Still, we have a choice. We could do it differently. Instead of getting caught up in this way, we can investigate pointing itself, with the understanding that the one who points and that which is being pointed to are both manifestations of the pointing activity.

It may seem that this suggestion does not get us anywhere. Don't the questions we ask about pointing immediately direct us back toward the structures that pointing presupposes? We have seen as much already: there is no act of pointing without a pointer and an object that we could call the point.

The difficulty seems to be that pointing itself is an act defined in a conceptual way. If we could keep the focus on the *activity* of pointing, the circumstances would appear very differently.

The structures that pointing depends on are there, but they are simply structures. We do not have to accept the reality or solidity of those structures. Instead, we can see them as moments in the dynamic of pointing. We can acknowledge this dynamic as what makes possible the appearance of what is pointed out.

Seen in this light, it makes sense to say that it is the luminosity of knowing that matters. What is known in the act of pointing out is in some sense secondary. This does not mean that we should ignore what is pointed out, which may after all have great significance for us. Instead, we can simply acknowledge that what is known in the act of pointing is the immediate expression of a more fundamental *knowingness*.

As we proceed through the stages of naming, interpreting, labeling, identifying, and placing, an appreciation for this fundamental knowingness can offer us vital support. It lets us bear in mind that the structures we take for granted have an 'always arising' and 'never established' nature. This holds even for those structures that seem to us beyond question. It is true for what arises and immediately passes away, but it is just as true for the fundamental truths of the regime in which we operate—the rules and roles by which our minds abide.

This regime is worth exploring in some detail, for it may have a role to play in why we know so little about ourselves and our origins—and why we are in such need of care.

Rules for Our Experience

Asking about the regime we inhabit and where it comes from lets us consider the building blocks of what is taken as reality. It also sets the stage for investigating the depiction of our identity. We see that the conditions for our experience have largely already happened before we are even aware experience is going on. This stimulates some basic questions: How do conditions interrelate and become what is taken as reality? And what governs these conditions?

To explore these questions, we could propose, a little playfully, that there are two strict rules involved in being ourselves.

Rule #1 for understanding our experience: *Every object needs a subject.* You can't have one without the other, and we could not have what we call 'reality' without them, either.

Under this rule, perception means that something appears *to us*. There is a full recognition that something is happening. At the moment an object appears, the subject is simultaneously there. Reality as we know it cannot make its presence felt without subjects and objects.

Rule # 2 for understanding our experience: *Without a 'from' there cannot be a 'to.'* This statement may need some unpacking: we could say that if something exists, it must have a 'from,' a beginning; and a 'to,' a projection forward, an abiding in time.

This rule is not only talking about the existence of objects in the world. We are trying to understand how objects appear *to* an observer. For anything to appear, there must be a relationship between a 'from' and a 'to.' 'To' has no function when there is no object: if the object is not there, there is no 'to.' So, every 'to' needs a 'from,' and every 'to' comes from a subject.

To take this a little further, we could say that the subject is the opposite of the object. The subject—the boss, the doer, the agent—is a 'from' that relates 'to' an object. The subject-object relation is set up right from the start. The appearance of an object requires a subject.

Once we are at this level, the self appears, and it starts to have experiences. We begin to establish meaningful internal connections. We are happy or not, we are healthy or not, we are in joy or in pain. Through repetition of these circulating 'froms' and 'tos', we develop an identity.

All these elements and stages come together to make experience. This is the cauldron in which experience is made.

When the input from impressions becomes overwhelming, we feel pressure. When it reaches a boiling point, we become confused, frustrated, or depressed.

Because our body and mind are in so many ways a mystery to us—a kind of unexplored continent—we are unaware of the conditions that might contribute to our sense of happiness or unhappiness. Our feelings and emotions may be related to different kinds of causes, from diet, exercise, the DNA structure from our parents, chemical balance, to myriad unknowns. We don't seem to know why we are happy or unhappy, and are unable to determine how the next moment will be.

Our lives seem governed by chance, as if each moment pops out of a random number generator. We don't know what number will come up next.

We are all accustomed to thinking of ourselves as subjects and owners, masters of all we survey, pointing 'out there' from 'in here.' Yet our certainty masks a great deal of confusion. When we play 'master' in this way, we are actually being obedient subjects who have deeply internalized the 'rules' of experience.

Pointing out the Rulers

Since we are the ones who point, we are likely to hold that what is most fundamental in any act of pointing out is—no surprise here—the one who points. This leads us to the aspect of ownership, which proves to be essential. In pointing out, we own what is pointed out. Even if we cannot assert any claim to possess what is being pointed to—for instance, a beautiful sunset—we still claim ownership of the experience of having seen what I am now pointing out.

Do we really need to include this dimension of ownership? It seems that we do. If there were no owner of experience, there would be no certainty about what is experienced, and we could not rely on it to function in a reliable way.

The identity of the owner is what gives continuity to experience. It establishes and solidifies experience as something that can be known, as a recognizable whole.

Put differently, we live out our lives within a regime that makes sense of what is so, and that regime functions only on the basis of claims to ownership. The regime itself has rulers, and the rulers govern. They set in motion the forces that lead or conduct the presupposed into being. A claim of ownership and control is present from the outset, and it works its way down through every facet of every appearance.

When we look for these rulers of the regime in our experience, we do not have to look very far. At the middle of experience, shaping it in well-defined ways, are *I* and *me* and *mine* and *mind.* These are the identified identifiers, the decision-makers and operators, who give shape and form and offer judgments. The rules and laws that establish existence depend on their activity, for they are the ones who frame distinctions, identify different parts and their interactions, and validate pro and con.

It is important that we not understand these structures in an overly personal way. No one is saying that I—this personal, individual me, with its history and personality—am somehow the secret sovereign of all I survey, as though I had a status no one else could claim. My point is different. Whatever our particular set of circumstances, every set of experiences—yours and mine alike—is assigned to an *owner at the center,* an identifier and decision-maker. That is how the regime works.

It seems helpful to refer to this ruler as multiple, as the cooperating entities of I and me and mine and mind. 'I' sorts through the endless manifestations, making decisions, assigning, and appropriating. 'I' plays the dominant role—it sets itself up as number one, first and foremost. Yet 'me' is also active, confirming that the work of 'I' is 'my' doing. 'Me' sets up the identity of 'I', and 'I' depends on the distinctions that 'me' makes.

To give an analogy: a tour guide cannot play her role unless there are tourists to guide. First they must show up; then they must confirm the tour guide's authority. Only then can the tour guide start to work. In the same way, 'me' affirms 'I's role. It lays out 'I's path and confirms its duties and responsibility. I may be the actor, the identified entity, but I also have no choice but to play the role that 'me' has confirmed.

In this way, 'I' depends on me, much as the actors on the stage need their audience if they are to be identified as actors. Given the conditions under which I and me operate, this means in part confirming 'I's physical embodiment, which 'I' is generally ready to identify as me. Having been identified, 'me' acknowledges: "Yes, I am." Without that acknowledgement, nothing will function as it should: the regime will stop making sense.

'Me' salutes 'I,' as a soldier salutes an officer. "Yes sir," says 'me,' and by that very act 'me' confirms that 'I' must take responsibility for how things are and for the role 'I' plays within that established 'reality'. Within that structure, 'mine' serves as well, making the necessary links and connections.

Yet this structure remains incomplete. Despite being the one at the center—the ultimate 'number one'—'I' has problems. In simple terms we could say that it is forever thirsty and hungry; that it longs for something that it does not know how to find. Incomplete, it seeks without success, now and for all time, always ill at ease.

Here we would expect 'me' to step in, to offer support, to make 'mine' what 'I' is missing. Yet 'me' is not up to the task. 'Me' cannot see what 'I' cannot do, for 'me' is not the actor; in the end, it has no way to solve the core problem—the hunger or the lack—around which 'I' structures its being.

We could put it this way: 'me' does not know how to care for 'I', just as 'I', in the end, does not know how to care for 'me'. The interaction of 'I' and 'me' is the central, governing connection, yet something is missing. A vital knowledge fails to cohere.

'I' has many tricks up its sleeve. It can dictate and simulate, it can copy and follow pre-existing patterns. Within a certain range of possibilities, it can improvise to arrive where it wants to be. But when these solutions are not enough, the final truth is that 'I' has no way to care for 'me', 'me' has no way to care for 'I', and 'mine' cannot make the link.

Mind Reflects on Caring

Asking how to care for I and me and mine, when they cannot care for one another, we are led to the mind. But what can we say about mind and its capacity to care? In the realm of experience in which we move and live, mind is so close. Perhaps it is the closest of all. Yet mind remains in many ways unknown. If we want to overcome that ignorance, or at least understand it more fully, we must look anew, with fresh eyes.

In the interaction of me and mine, mind seems to play a neutral role. We act, and thanks to mind our actions are reflected back to us. We perceive and think, and mind is like the mirror in which the objects of our perceptions and thoughts manifest.

Mind makes its contribution to experience through the sensory faculties and their individual modes of consciousness. It shows and it shares; it determines the 'yes' of this and the 'no' of that. It determines the rules by which I and me and mine play their games, and it judges the outcome. It offers a logic of existence and appearance, as well as their opposites, and it gives us a sense of what is true—what is really so.

That is not all. What appears to mind, in mind, or through mind is not in itself neutral. Mind can go toward the 'joy-ness' of joy, or the 'pain-ness' of pain. It can allow confusion to reign, together with uncertainty, dullness, or ambivalence. Mind can take us on a journey into dark and unknown places, reflecting fundamental dimensions of experience that we know all too well.

In all these operations, what can be said of mind itself? Is it affected by what it reflects, or is it truly more like a mirror? When we consider mind and mind's operations, we quickly realize that for mind to play the role it does, mind itself must be transparent, like a very pure crystal. It is only through such transparency, operating as the fundamental of mind, that mind is able to reveal the forms and images that constitute our perceptions and thoughts. It is only in its openness that it can present such appearances to I and me. As images proliferate, mind creates the conditions that shape what will appear. It offers its own unique knowledge.

It may sound as though this amounts to a kind of perfect neutrality after all, but that is not so. Transparency does not mean absence. In fact, the opposite is more nearly true. In presenting patterns and appearances, mind manifests a dynamics of care.

This is not the limited kind of care that 'I' can offer 'me' and 'me' can offer 'mine', the kind of care we may know from our daily dealings.

The care that mind manifests has a deeper quality. No matter what specifics may manifest, positive or negative, mind's caring is informed by radiant luminosity. In the end it is inseparable from knowingness.

Obstacles to Care

We live in a culture whose values sometimes seem opposed to care. We pursue our professions or responsibilities almost obsessively, making it difficult to communicate at the level where care can manifest. As children grow to maturity, they are trained in various ways to be cynical about their leaders and skeptical of the very existence of authentic caring. They learn that most people care only about their own selfish aims or the welfare of those who are close to them.

The education that the young receive also does little to support the importance of care, for they are given little to care about and care for. Taught history in only a superficial way, they learn relatively little about the great achievements of this civilization and others that have contributed so much to the world. Naturally they end up focusing on their own personal situation: family, career, work, and a loose network of shifting friendships.

Because no one cares, important aspects of our human heritage simply disappear.

Ominous Examples

I see this danger in my own country of Tibet, now under foreign rule, where study of a fourteen-hundred-year-old tradition of wisdom and compassion is systematically discouraged, and even the Tibetan language is not taught in schools.

For me, a symbol of such disregard for what has real value is the loss, year after year, of indigenous languages that are no longer spoken or taught: I have been told that on average a language disappears every two weeks.

When it comes to the natural environment, the same patterns prevail. Again and again we are told that the planet is in danger, that rapid and irreversible change is on the horizon. Some people respond, but the majority hold back, waiting for someone else to do something. From time to time an emergency bursts forth, and then people take action, but after a while we settle back into the same old routines. When the next emergency arises, we are caught by surprise.

There are countless other examples that demonstrate the same systemic lack of caring. Poverty increases year by year, and gradually we learn to take it for granted. Violence erupts in our schools and on the streets, and nothing changes. Whole populations around the globe face famine or warfare, and everyone agrees that something must be done. Yet those who care seem powerless to do anything about it, while those in power seem to operate with a different set of cares and concerns.

On the material level, we may lack the knowledge to evaluate what is truly good for us. Go shopping, and there are literally millions of things to buy. How much knowledge do we have of where they come from, how they were made, and what impact they will have on us or the environment? Even when products are known to be toxic, manufacturers have no incentive to make changes if it will have a negative impact on their profits.

While this culture has developed truly valuable technologies, a lack of care means that we sometimes fail to see clearly the larger context. For instance, there are many drugs available today that can help relieve symptoms or even cure diseases. Yet it sometimes happens that drugs that give relief in the short term prove poisonous to the body in the long term. In other cases, drugs that relieve pain can sometimes lead to addiction and eventually despair.

It is remarkable that in a society like ours, with so many advantages and such vast resources available to it, the rate of suicide continues to increase.

Clearly, we face serious dysfunction as a society—with little evidence that our situation is going to improve. But this is not a moment to despair. Instead, we could understand it as a call to arms—or a cry for help.

Investing Our Lives

We don't know all the causal connections that determine our experience, whether we look at chemical structures, mental and cultural structures, or emotional structures. All of these have their own beginnings and causal contributions to our well-being. Subtle internal changes affect our responses prior to our full awareness of our perceptions. We can see that there are waves of pressure, duties that differ culture to culture, and temptations specific to certain environments. With this in mind, we need to consider carefully how to best invest our time and energy.

American culture centers on a vision of individual success and prosperity for us and our loved ones. From an early age we are taught that to succeed requires a good education, a good job, money, power, reputation, being well-liked, and having youthful vitality. All are elements of the American dream, part of what it means to be happy. The dream feeds identity and provides us with a vision of the highest good: to protect and promote pleasure for the self and those immediately within our circle.

Commonly, people invest in pleasure and the senses without questioning if this investment is wise. I am deemed happy if I enjoy my youth, am proud of my achievements, and if I have had many great experiences that I have crossed off my bucket list.

All the while, chemicals are moving in the body, continually changing, being replaced, and eventually aging —glands run down, energy fades, skin loses its luster. If we have a big investment in the pleasures of our senses, our investment will inevitably stop paying dividends. If we invest in the body, its pleasures will not last; in the end, only memories and fantasies remain. We don't have a choice: the body changes. If we invest exclusively in youthful energy and value only these external, transient shows of beauty and power, when the time comes, we will have no internal resources left.

If we consider our life as a journey, intertwined with the vast processes of the universe that have made our existence possible—from the elements we share with the stars to the moving alchemy of our bodies and our actions within human culture—we can ask how we are using this heritage. What have we received for all our effort at achieving fame, money, good experiences, and relationships?

How much are we getting back from our investments?

Some people might object, "I have my activities. I am proud of my accomplishments. I have my family. Life is beautiful." But all these are only memories, present-tense declarations of what has already passed. In truth, the investment is already draining away.

Operating at a Steady Loss

Someone else might reply with a shrug, "My investment got lost, but that is the way of the world. All human beings are in the same situation. Whatever. I have no solution or choice." The stock market goes up or down. We have no choice about that. In the end, we are much the same. We all end up like bankrupt companies.

This has been the way of human beings for all time. Our lives do not seem to be any different from those who have gone before. We have made great strides in improving our living conditions; we have clean water, mechanical and electrical wonders. We can correct poor vision with eyeglasses or laser surgery, and straighten crooked teeth. We have made progress in a technical sense, but we can't seem to fix the inner structure of unhappiness.

We cannot ignore these circumstances of our reality. Yet we don't want to give in to despair. Our life journey has been an investment of time, history, education, and generations of effort. It would be a terrible waste to give in to gloom and unhappiness. Surely this cannot be the final word on the matter.

Duty of Care

In modern, Western countries like America, there are things "you just need": things to be, and things to do. We need to secure our interests; we need to take care of our families.

> *I need to do my job. I need to drive this car, clean this house, pick up these kids. These things have to happen! Then I'm tired. Then, I need some 'Me-time.' Don't bother me when I'm eating!*

There is no time to evaluate how much of this effort is meaningful.

Look, I'm trying my best, but I have duties, responsibilities. I can't think about this right now.

I have to keep on doing this. I have to keep on being myself.

It seems we must keep fulfilling our duties until the investments we have made are exhausted. But what happens then? We need to assess the real value of our way of life.

This means we urgently need to pay attention to caring. We need to pay attention to the confusion, the dissatisfaction, and loneliness that is all around us. We need to care for and about each other and act with the best intentions.

With caring, we could develop a better way of being there when our friends and families need us. We could be a stronger presence in the world that needs so much of us. We might be able to grow the patience and tolerance to accept the challenges we face, even the misunderstandings of those around us. Even if they don't return our care, we might have the inner resources to continue caring.

At the very least, even if our caring for others made only a limited impact, we could commit ourselves to having no more suffering ourselves. True caring requires inward cooperation—a coalition of thoughts, feelings and sensing. Nothing stops us from experiencing and expressing that kind of care.

Consider the possibilities: we could take care of ourselves and let go of dissatisfaction, loneliness, and regrets. Gradually we could embody a deep and real understanding of caring. We could show we are *better off caring.* We could even become models of caring.

We may not have enough money or power to help great numbers of people, but we could embody this knowledge of caring. We could manifest practical caring in word and gesture, impression and expression.

We could make a difference.

Mindful of this, it is time to ask ourselves, very seriously:

> *How much meaning and satisfaction do our actions bring?*
>
> *What have we gotten back from our investment?*
>
> *Have we healed our hearts?*
>
> *Have we known a depth of love?*
>
> *Have we benefited others?*

Urgent Care

*We must be ready to acknowledge
that the world is urgently in need of care.*

Uncertain of Care

It is easy to feel overwhelmed by the pressures and obligations of modern life. It seems as if everyone is focused on comparisons and competition. We feel pressure to make money, get a good education, find an interesting job, and provide for the family. Even with our loved ones, it is easy to become lost, to let the initial bloom of caring fade into duties and responsibilities. We get caught up in the dictates of our situation and scarcely have time to reflect on what we value or the quality of our lives.

As we take up our particular goals and obligations, our sense of caring focuses more narrowly on these pursuits. We close our eyes to the pain that this restricted focus causes to ourselves and others. We become absorbed in external responsibilities, competition, and a pursuit of personal security, and we tend to forget what is important to our sense of value. We might say we *need* to take care of our family, our jobs, our obligations: "That is what I care about." All the while the quality of our caring is limited, pressured, and not very nourishing at an immediate level.

We get caught up in comparison and competition, and never allow the small blossom of caring to grow for ourselves or others. Distracted and lacking deep connections, we grow lonely. Lacking inner knowledge, we close down. We don't know how to develop the qualities of caring that would allow us to open up with skill and joy to ourselves and the world.

Caring in a Crowded World

The modern world can be strikingly distant and impersonal. And *crowded*—full of people we don't know, with whom we are nevertheless in constant contact.

Walk down the street in any city or large town; enter any shopping mall, and there is a mass of strangers in numbers that would have astonished our ancestors. We move among these strangers without making eye-contact; we speak to them as little as possible, and what we say is usually confined to business. We buy our goods, say our thanks, and part ways.

This circumstance—that we are alone in a crowded world—can leave us feeling very lonely.

But this condition is not only something we experience among strangers. While loved ones often try to support us, we may feel poorly understood at home, or even alienated from our own families. Friends can help us in time of need—and yet the experiences we have within our social networks often give rise to anxiety, frustration, and resentment.

For many of us, the same crowded and lonely qualities mark our inner lives. We may feel overwhelmed by our feelings, and struggle to accommodate our own thoughts.

It almost feels as if we are losing our capacity to care—as if we are in danger of losing caring itself, because it has become so much harder to rely on anyone, even ourselves.

Ever-Moving Mystery

If we are honest with ourselves, a brief look inside will confirm that our feelings and the workings of our minds are not really predictable. We are not entirely sure where we are going, or where we have been. Looking back, we can see how different we were ten or even five years ago. The cells that make up our bodies have been replaced several times over the course of our personal histories; the chemical structures have shifted. Even the particles that make up our bodies have changed.

Over those years our minds have changed as well. Old beliefs have been tested and revised. Old attitudes have been discarded—or they have grown rigid with time, making us defensive and awkward in unexpected ways.

There are also more subtle changes, changes to our spirit that are hard even to put into words.

But how many of us really accept this simple truth? When we look in a mirror, we see ourselves *today*. We say, "This is who I am": real, recognizable, ordinary, and somehow *unchanging*—the face we see today much like the one we saw yesterday. We don't often consider that the face we see in the mirror today is already becoming tomorrow's memory.

Driving down a highway that runs along the bank of a river, we notice the stream rolling beside us. It seems like a constant companion, an unchanging reality. But the river is also moving.

Everything in our lives—inside and outside us—is moving, just like that.

To our eyes, it all *looks* like it's holding still, or developing very slowly, like a tree. But if we were to change how we measure that growth, we would discover that the world is changing with startling speed—and so are we.

Think of how fast our planet is moving through space. We didn't see the changes, we don't feel the movement—but our planet, our solar system, and our galaxy are all steadily changing position with respect to the rest of the universe.

Understanding causes and conditions lets us trace and source every form of matter, every being that arises. But can we trace the space that seems to serve as the basis for this activity? The foundation of space itself, the origin of the energy that gave rise to the universe: that point is so far unknown, and perhaps unknowable.

It turns out to be hard to define the basis or foundation of what exists—the point on which we appear to stand, a starting point or resting point that our being here at all seems to require.

Unstable, insubstantial: that seeming foundation is more like the echo of a voice, a transient perception, a dream or the appearance of a dream. When we look at it all, it seems like a magical world, a piece of fiction or theater. More than that: when we regard ourselves doing the looking, we discover that we ourselves might be players. We're not only the audience, but the actors, part of this magic show of space, staged by mind for mind.

It may be that the magician, the active, projecting mind, is also a magical body. The mystery moves both ways, showing itself to itself, forward and backward, in dimensions our ordinary perceptions have no way to reach.

We could imagine these mystery-moments as *ocean ripples*: arising, moving through the water of our life-experience, and passing away. Some repeat, and some interact, creating new ripples, new patterns of behavior. But while we may appreciate that idea at the intellectual level, we often feel unprepared when new ripples come.

Every painful thought, every emotion, every up and down: we take it all so seriously, all the pain, sorrow, loneliness, agitation, and pride. Maybe we try to reason that these feelings are transitory. But it is very hard to say, "These sensations are already memories," and actually mean it. For now, at least, they seem very present.

There is beauty and wonder here, but most of us have not had any experiences that can show us how to live in and with that magic—how to practice it ourselves. Instead, the mystery often feels more like a blank wall: we can't get beyond it, and we can't see what it hides.

Cause: Unknown

Most of us cannot trace the causal connections that establish where we came from, or how we came to be the people we have become. Yet the Western world is good at finding the causes of things—the how of it all. Perhaps we could leverage that skill, examine what provokes our suffering, and learn that it is not accidental.

If we understood better, we could trace back the how of how suffering, loneliness and despair come about for all of us.

For it seems that we don't know how to stop our experiences from turning sour; we don't really know how these thoughts bubble up. How did we come to be lonely? There is little by way of education about the causes and conditions—no instructions that clarify how we came to believe in our thoughts as anything more than just bubbles that arise and will eventually pop.

We don't know the whole story, but we can see that thoughts and feelings are connected with language, and we can see the way identity arises within the subject-object relation. On a deep level, we are made by concepts, and our identity has its roots in interpretation.

In some deep and inaccessible space in some almost untraceable instant of time, subject and object seem to automatically pop up whenever a perception is formed. Something is happening—even before thought and feeling are fully formed. The sense-doors are opened, and we have already been captured. Once subject and object are connected, there is an unavoidable, irrevocable response. We like or don't like what appears. We say 'yes' or 'no.' That is how we connect with experience.

But we don't know how to contact the very instant that experience takes shape and form, or the conditions that allow experience to arise.

Unclear about how any of the events of our lives have taken shape, we have only a dim sense of our history. Our memories go back only so far, and they are spotty in many places. Reflecting on the path our existence has taken through time, we reach a point beyond which it seems impossible to trace any further causes. Uncertain of our own origins, we are likewise unsure of what comes next, after the short span of our lives is complete.

Holding on for Dear Life

Perhaps this is why we hold on to what pops up: what is judged good or bad is *possessed* as good or bad. We want to hold on to the feeling even if it is poisonous, even if thoughts make trouble. We would rather hold on to our pain and establish an identity.

For example, we sometimes recognize that we are angry, or feel inadequate, embarrassed and ashamed. And we cling to this identification: "Yes," we say, "I know this. *This* is true. My feelings come up, sometimes without warning, but they are mine, they are real, and I accept them." We want to possess them, as fleeting and as bubble-like as they are.

If we understood how to care for ourselves, we would let these feelings and thoughts go, for they are not only limiting, they are toxic. They sicken us and poison our experience.

If we truly care for ourselves, surely we don't want to make more suffering and trouble for ourselves, or become 'intoxicated' with pain. We don't want an empty life, lived out in loneliness. Yet we hold on to the pain and isolation.

> *I have problems. I am in trouble.*
> *That is my reality.*

Living in this way, I fear we are losing more and more of our humanity. We develop technologically, stretching farther and farther; we work incessantly, running faster and faster until exhaustion comes. The goals of our work seem to serve the rules that have been set up and are not supporting our well-being.

People operating in our materialistic, competitive society sometimes reach a point of saying, "I'm done competing. I'm out." The system of worldly rewards provides little nourishment or meaning even for those who are successful on its terms. As many of us can attest, the work we do gets old quickly if it has no intrinsic meaning.

Others of us, less fortunate, without prospects or opportunities, just give up.

"I don't care" manifests as resentment and translates into "I can't keep up" or "I don't understand" or "It's dead to me." Some of us turn to drugs or alcohol to manage our constant pain and anxiety.

The Only Caring We Know

The anxiety and apathy that we find in ourselves and others could be a result of the way we experience our impermanence—the mysterious, unstable character of our existence as sentient beings.

We have very little understanding of impermanence, and no reliable guides to teach us how to relate to it. Without better ways to work with the ups and downs of our journey, we learn to withdraw into ourselves, to barricade ourselves inside, to turn our minds to escapist fantasies or our own inner preoccupations. But this approach to the instability we feel, inside and out, will not let us make the most of our journey.

Instead, we are at the mercy of the anxiety-laden 'I,' 'me,' and 'self.' The mind clings to 'mine,' holding onto these positions as tightly as it can—but they are uncertain signposts in a strange landscape.

Lost and alone, in the private spaces of our minds, we suffer in ways we can never quite share, even with our friends and loved ones.

> *Today hurts—it hurts! It eats up my life. Just getting by takes all my effort and energy. There's nothing mystical or mysterious about it: this situation is real. I know what I'm talking about! I know what I'm feeling.*
>
> *This sense of myself, my pain—it's all I have!*

This is the world according to me, according to my mind, to my self. Don't patronize me, don't tell me I'm suffering—I already know!

I know that I'm hungry. I know I'm cold, angry, lonely! I know I can't get my needs met. That's why I act out: at least I can do that, and more. I can show you my suffering. I can tell you it needs to stop.

That's my reality. And this cry—this expression of my pain—is the only way I know how to care.

When this pain takes over, we can become myopically focused on ourselves and our concerns, even ignoring the pain of others.

I need this more than you do! I've suffered enough! Even if it harms you, it's my right! Besides, what have you ever done for me? This little bit of good, I need it!

What else am I supposed to do? What else is there? All I know how to do is this! I have to be a person and deal with this situation. That's what's real! At least I know THAT.

Can you blame me if I try to get away from the needs of other people? Can you blame me if I don't pay attention to my own needs? I can't ever get them fulfilled. The best I can do is distract myself. A little fun, a little pleasure. I need it—more than you!

I have to have it, because I deserve it. I deserve it
because I do my best every day to play this part.
I work so hard, and nobody understands!
Nobody cares.

We live our lives imprisoned by the dictatorship of our beliefs, patterns set up and imparted to us since we were children, whether we like them or not.

This is life. This is the way it is.
This is the way I am.

We labor under this yoke, living in a world cast and modeled according to the dictates of a mind that has been taught to believe fervently in its own isolation.

In this world, we all grow up lonely; we all grow up needing more care.

Without the knowledge of caring—without a clear understanding of what 'caring' could mean—we struggle with one another, convinced that for one of us *to have*, the other must *not have*. We become entrenched in mistreating ourselves and others.

Our inability to care has consequences, playing out in the world around us and in the inner world of our thoughts and feelings, as we sense our inner potentials slipping away—and watch generation after generation go on to enact the same painful patterns.

Maybe we want something different—but when we try to envision something else—something more nourishing—our own minds, obedient subjects of this uncaring regime, become our worst enemies.

> *Could we... could we get some real nourishment?*
> *"Yeah, right! How would you do that?"*
> *Well... I don't know.*
> *"If you don't know, then just be quiet!"*

If you've ever felt this way, you are not alone.

A Different Kind of Caring

Think of all the human beings that have existed on this planet since we first emerged on the African plains. Think of your family and friends, your teachers and community leaders; think of all the faces you see around you.

Reflect on the suffering you can see in those faces. Who can help with this? What can be done? Is anyone really looking at this problem?

> *It's true. We take for granted that it has to be like this. But I think we really are in crisis.*

Is there any wisdom, any guidance to turn to? Perhaps we need a new way to conduct this business of being human—a new constitution, a new set of beliefs. We might benefit from learning more about caring, about ourselves.

I don't care!
No... that's not true. I do *care.*
But it's so hard to accept... there's so much
suffering. I don't want to look... I want to
avoid this. I care, but I'm trying not to care.

To care, we need to look.

It can be hard to look. We feel hesitant, overwhelmed, because it's painful. It's hard to realize how many of us are suffering. We find it so difficult because a lot of us have not developed the layers of inner strength that would let us confront the suffering of others. It is like trying to walk on a stony road without shoes.

Wisdom, self-respect and self-appreciation can help provide the support that makes us stronger. Then we will be more able to help others.

Learning how to care, therefore, starts with ourselves. Once we have acknowledged our urgent need for care, we can begin by taking care of our own body and mind. We can learn the vehicle of caring inside and out.

When we are sure that we are capable of handling the ups and downs of our own journey, then we have something to offer.

Not everyone will have a chance to go deeply into caring, to learn caring through and through for themselves. Most people are wrapped up in just trying to make it to the next day. Very few of us, really, find help, instructions, solutions: most of us have only hope to go on.

When we think of how rare it is for human beings to discover the depths of caring, it will better help us recognize how precious our own opportunity is. Are we up for the task? What we learn about caring is not for our sake alone.

On Behalf of All

We are the people we are thanks to our parents, our teachers, and everyone who extended care to us as we were growing up. Even if we can't always see or acknowledge the care we received, the fact that we are here, alive, means that someone helped us when we could not help ourselves.

On behalf of the helpers, we must take care of ourselves—we must care for this being they poured out their own energy to protect. For their sake, we must honor their efforts, and keep ourselves alive and well.

And for the sake of all who continue to suffer, we need to relate to ourselves with kindness, to support ourselves and care for ourselves even when the world around us lets us down.

Above all, we must protect our hearts from disillusionment and resentment. We must not decide that because someone is unkind to us, we should stop caring for ourselves.

*The world needs to see what it's done to me.
If I hurt myself, then they'll be sorry. But it
will be too late! I'll be gone, and it will be
their turn to hurt.*

This attitude is common, and it's important to think about its consequences carefully. Many of us are in pain and have been through great hardship. No one appreciates being told that they are playing the victim, or that their suffering is some kind of performance. Such a thought seems to minimize and dismiss the sufferer's pain.

Nevertheless, by hurting ourselves deliberately to 'get back' at those who hurt us, we do not heal ourselves; instead, we create only more pain.

*But you're being unfair. I'm not doing anything
unusual—everybody who's ever been mistreated
suffers like that! And we all hurt ourselves all
the time. I'm only doing what literally everyone
else does.*

We treat ourselves this way because it is what we have become accustomed to. We model our behavior on the behavior of others, whether it is parents or peers.

*I copied them; I followed their model. What
else could I do? My mind, my feelings,
everything got taught to follow the pattern.
My whole environment reinforced that message!
Everything was telling me, "embody, adopt,*

accept it!" It's built into my language,
my ideas, my whole identity!

Think of someone you love, someone you admire—
even if it's a hero of yours whom you've never actually
met. Ask yourself if you would want to see that wonderful person go down such a dark and lonely road. When
we look at those behaviors in those we love, we can
see very clearly that they are harmful, not behaviors to
emulate. Can we make a change? Maybe we don't have
to go down that same road anymore.

This approach to caring by starting with ourselves
may seem alien.

How could taking care of ourselves help anyone
else? Isn't it selfish? Wouldn't it be best to direct
that energy outward to those who need it more?

But it is the right place to start. We can't always help
others, but at least we can guarantee our own well-
being at a very deep level—the kind of well-being that
can help us weather the storms and work more creatively with the hardship we experience. If we can learn
this, we can treat others better. We can at least ensure
that we are not contributing to their misery.

More than that—we stand a chance of helping other
people learn the same thing. This is the only way we
can make a real dent in the suffering and neglect that
so many of us endure.

Done Pretending

This modern world—especially in the lands of the West—is full of dramas, full of dreams. We all play along, taking starring roles inside our own minds. But we didn't write these plays ourselves.

We label up our experiences and feelings exactly as we've been taught to do. When we learned to talk, to be human, we also learned to play our roles.

We learned: I am not you. We learned: I want this; I do not want that. This is what *happiness* looks like; this is what *sadness* feels like. Without even realizing it, we obey many rules that have to do with *being myself.* And we follow the rules of the drama when we relate to others.

Every time we communicate, we communicate according to the rules of this play of mind. And the play is reinforced, the rules and roles taken so seriously that we forget anyone is playing a part at all.

We are largely unaware of the seductive, subliminal power of the play—and that makes us vulnerable. Our thoughts and sense-impressions can be easily influenced by these pervasive dramas. We are not always aware how this takes place, or even that it has occurred at all.

> *No, no, these are my real feelings. This is how I always feel when something bad happens. There's a reason I feel uncomfortable: someone was angry with me, someone was unkind.*

… What do you mean, I got tricked…?

As soon as the drama appears, we pick it up. We recognize it, identify it, and identify *with it*. Then it's caught in our head. We're in the mouth of the crocodile. Once we're in there, it is very hard to get out again.

> *I can't help it: I understand language. I receive the message. I can't just ignore my culture, this way of life, this feeling! It seems so urgent, I have to participate… and then I get captured.*
>
> *We call this mess "reality," and then…*
>
> *And then, it becomes impossible to change.*

Our best knowledge has not always been able to take care of us, to console and uplift us. Most of our education follows the same rules; it is another part of the play. It reinforces the patterns we see. Even the brightest thinkers among us do not seem immune; even our finest philosophers seem baffled by suffering, and severely limited in what they can do to help.

It almost seems as though the more the world develops, the more quickly it moves, the more suffering, too, develops and rapidly spreads.

> *I wish I could say, "You're exaggerating just for effect." But I can see the truth. This painful way of life isn't unique to me. It's not just happening in my family or my home town. There are signs of the same struggle all over the world.*

57

Most of the time, we deal with the pain by trying to pretend we are OK. Even wealthy, successful, famous people pretend, but they have problems that are sometimes very serious. Still they must keep on being pretenders—carry on smiling, because their roles require it. We may not be famous, but are we so different?

This pretending has not served us well. We need to be real with ourselves. We need to promise never to hurt ourselves. We need to ensure that heart and head are protected from our own negativity: never harmed, never hit, pushed or poked, pinched or squashed. We must decide not to chew on ourselves anymore.

Because when we mistreat ourselves long enough, sometimes the point is reached where we don't care anymore, about anything or anybody.

Mission-Critical

It's important to take a moment to reflect on the seriousness of our situation.

So many of us are in pain and confusion, desperately afraid of loss. So many are confined by the dictates of identity, which has very little to offer by way of beauty, knowledge, or healing. Stuck with the demands of identity, caught up, with everybody else, in ways of being that discourage caring, many of us have sacrificed our inner sense of what matters most.

But no matter what has happened to us, we are still

thinking, feeling human beings. And deep within us we have the power to care, for ourselves and for others.

Our experiences can be more than a source of painful memories. They can be part of an important mission— a path that has been walked by humanity's most dedicated healers, its master-rescuers, great heroes both known and unknown, famous and anonymous.

What made them so great? Just this: *they cared* for all sentient beings. They knew *how* to care, how to release the people around them from pain and loneliness. They understood how to transform confusion into confidence, kindness, and unshakable awareness.

We need to learn that wisdom and that confidence. We need a way to secure these treasures for ourselves. This is a value that has been recognized by human beings across history; this is the heart of religion, the essence of philosophy. These could be our personal treasures. With them, we could help ourselves; gradually, perhaps we could help many others.

All right. I'm tired of pretending. I want to try.

Exercise: Morning Promise

Every morning, before you begin your day, look in the mirror. Regarding yourself kindly and patiently, promise yourself that you will take care of yourself, no matter what: looking after yourself body and mind, spirit and heart.

PART THREE

Careful Attention

It is time to take a closer look at caring—
for how we understand caring will ultimately
decide whether we are capable of caring.

Precious Life

Time seems to be full of cycles and repetitions. We mark these cycles, noticing when weeks and hours pass; rarely do we stop to notice that each of these moments is unique and irreplaceable as it disappears.

It takes attention to recognize this fundamental fact of our lives: the time that's gone will not return. Until we discover this truth for ourselves, we can't unlock the real potentials of our *juncture*, our own unique, individual moment, when we are embodied in time.

> *When I pay attention to my life, I discover that it's short, much shorter than I thought. It's my chance to do something meaningful, and it's slipping away.*

I think there might be great potential here, but I know it can easily be wasted.

Is that what I want?

This recognition that life is precious is at the heart of caring.

This time, I will not be put off, dissuaded, distracted. This time, I will stay faithfully with my precious present moment.

The Power of Caring

Once we understand the urgent need for care, a unique opportunity arises. It is unique, for it makes no demands. There is no new knowledge to gain, no difficult topics to master. The heart of care has no structure at all: it arises freely and directly out of experience.

With care, all is well; everything is all right. We are free and intrinsically healthy. Our gestures, our expressions, and our impressions reflect caring's power. The depth of thought is inseparable from vastness of feeling, from love and ever more caring.

There are methods we can practice, exercises that can develop these qualities, but in the end, it is simply a matter of care.

Even when our stories seem to leave little room for care, it comes through all the same, in ways both clearly visible and out of view. Socially, we may care for others who lack the basics of sustenance. Philosophically, we may care for the inquiry that leads toward insight. Leaders care for the success of their undertakings and for those they lead. Religion cares for the welfare of the soul or the suffering of all who are born to die. Art cares for beauty and perhaps for instruction. The self cares for its own projects and for preserving its own identity.

Not all these forms of care express equally its unbounded power. Yet however it manifests, care has the power to transform. Ask what someone cares about and how they manifest their care, and you will know how that person relates to wisdom and compassion, love and respect.

Care is a vital aspect of our journey through life, sustaining goodness and rightness and supporting ways of life rich in satisfaction and positivity. When we care, we find meaning in all that we do, and we act in uncontrived ways to ensure that meaning will continue to inform our lives.

Caring naturally spreads out in ripples that affect the lives of others. When I care for you, you are more likely to care for me. When we care as a community, our caring affects our environment, the steps we take to assure the well-being of future generations, the welfare of those with whom we interact, and the dynamics through which we pass on our best values and understanding to posterity.

Rediscovering Lost Caring

If we lose the ability to care, we lose all of these benefits. We may start by not caring about the welfare of others, but in the end, we have no way to care even for ourselves. The thoughts and concepts that pass through our minds and the sensations that course through our bodies are confined and constricted, with no power to sustain what is positive.

Of course, none of this may manifest on the surface. It is possible for someone who cannot care, or whose ability to care has been shut down, to live a life that looks from outside to be successful and prosperous. On the inside, however, there is no joy, no sense of fulfilment. All is bleak. We can also trace this link in the opposite direction: for where there is unhappiness in any of its countless forms and manifestations, we can be sure that the ability to care has somehow been lost.

When we cannot care, we cannot take care of ourselves, and then life becomes chaotic, restless, and useless. Whatever the fruits of our efforts, they mean nothing to us. Whatever acknowledgement we receive cannot reach us or bring us comfort. Whatever nourishment we strive for turns to dust in our mouths. Each day is filled with numbing routine or disordered uncertainties. We cannot guide ourselves, cannot benefit others, and cannot find the motivation to reach for higher goals. We cannot find it within ourselves to plan and make decisions, to reach out to others, or to bring stability and order to our own disordered lives.

If I do not care, I do not belong. I begin to lose my humanity and my knowingness. But we do not always realize when we have become inured to care and unable to care for others.

When I do not care, I do not see. In the end I turn away from knowledge and knowingness, abandoning my birthright as a human being. My awareness fades into darkness and I stumble along with no aim and no sense of purpose. Living in this way, I bring harm to others without even intending to do so, and I gain no lasting benefit for myself.

But it is not until we recognize that we do not know how to care, or have lost the ability to do so, that the opportunity for change presents itself.

Knowing I do not care, I see that I have the choice: I can learn to care. I can learn to open myself to the possibilities for beauty, friendship, and meaningful action that life offers.

The signs of such a transformation are not difficult to see. When a stranger reaches out to me, I can respond with kindness, for caring opens my heart to others. I behave in new ways, showing respect and love. I appreciate whatever enters my life: from the chemical and biological interactions that have brought me into being and sustain me, to the creative imagination that finds expression in my thoughts and speculations.

Caring manifests in every moment of our lives. We may have learned to think in terms of caregivers and caretakers: nurses and janitors, social workers and teachers. Now, however, we realize that we, too, have a responsibility to care, together with the opportunities that come from caring. I can care for humanity and for all living beings. I can care for the future of this planet and the well-being of my neighbors, my friends, and my dear ones.

Care and Knowledge

We sometimes imagine that care and knowledge are at odds. We assign knowledge to the realm of facts and caring to the realm of feelings, and we make the assumption that reliable knowledge must be entirely separated from feelings. To care, in this understanding, is to open ourselves up to the possibility of bias and error.

In practice, however, this view makes little sense. We can see this when we look at the work of scientists, understood in this culture as the great custodians of knowledge. Science has learned so much in the past two centuries, leading to remarkable technologies and healing medical treatments, among countless other discoveries that have transformed our lives. It has also given us profound insights into the earliest moments of the universe, mastering methods that can derive new knowledge from tiny fragments of information.

At the same time, there is much that science does not know, from dark energy and dark matter to the workings of gravity and the causes of many deadly diseases, not to mention the great mysteries that surround the arising of consciousness.

The link between these two domains—the known and the unknown—is care.

Knowledge arises from the activities of scientists because they are trained to proceed with care. Each experiment is carefully thought out, each study care-fully designed to eliminate as best as possible the factors that could distort findings or stand in the way of achieving significant results.

Scientific care operates on another, perhaps more fundamental level. There is a caricature of the theoretical scientist according to which she does not care what use is made of her discoveries. Yet even the most abstract inquiry depends on proceeding with remarkable care in the design and implementation of experiments or protocols, as well as in analyzing results.

Nor is that all. Often scientists care deeply about advancing their field of inquiry and about the pursuit of knowledge. Like philosophers and creative artists, scientists care about what they are doing. This is one reason they are meticulous in what they do and how they do it. Because they care about the goals they pursue, they dedicate themselves completely, even when the research they pursue is limited in its scope and arcane in its implications. Intent on their work, they respond to the rhythms of the situation they encounter, and they create and compile accordingly. At no stage do they divorce care from knowledge. Each supports the other.

In our own everyday lives, the care with which we enact our most noble impulses reflects directly the inherent knowingness of mind, along with the infinite capacity of the mind to reflect appearance. Through care, we discover our destiny and awaken to our goals. We learn how to make our lives meaningful. The knowledge we rely on and the quality of our conduct are equally shaped by care. There is care for friends and family, care for the self, and care for the energy that allows us to manifest in time and space. The deeper levels of path, vision, and the body-mind interplay also arise in care.

Valuing Caring

When we investigate the conditions that make caring possible, we recognize that knowingness is the key. It starts with insights that may come readily. When I understand more deeply the countless conditions and circumstances that have led to my being here in this time and this place, I realize how interconnected I am with my environment and with other living beings, and care arises naturally. I find myself thinking of the past and of the future. Sensitive to how I and those I care about came to be, and where we are headed, I act to ensure a more positive and healing future.

In the history of humanity, the ability to care has been honored and cultivated in many ways. The great professions, whose best representatives are recognized in one form or another in all societies—religious leaders, political rulers, and moral exemplars; teachers, healers, and guides—come into being to express different kinds of caring. In each culture, generation after generation thrives only because care shapes the conduct of groups and individuals alike. Parents make care for their children the center of their lives, and people everywhere find ways to manifest their care within the larger community. Where this is not so, society suffers. Without care, it cannot long endure.

We may not have the power to address the problems that confront society on a large scale: the threat of nuclear weapons, war and hostility among nations, growing inequality, lasting damage to our beloved planet. Yet we do have the power to care. When we care for ourselves, our fellow beings, and the world we live in, we can develop greater awareness. Because we care for the fate of future generations, we can learn from the lessons of the past, investigate what is happening now, and act with regard to the future consequences of what we do. We do not need to speculate about what happens when people do not care: we can see it in the records of our own culture and the suffering that every past generation has experienced.

Exercise: Caring Beliefs

Take about twenty minutes to write, reflecting on what you really believe caring is, how it works, and what it can do. The object of this exercise is not to ultimately conclude we are going about caring in the wrong way. Rather, the point is to clarify what we inwardly believe is true about caring and get a closer look at those beliefs. When we can see them more plainly we can decide if we need to reconsider what we believe.

Exploration: What We Believe About Caring

When we start to pay attention to caring, we may make some important discoveries. We have a chance to discover our beliefs about caring: what we think caring really is, and whether we think caring is even possible. Depending on what they are, our beliefs can severely constrain our ability to give and receive care.

Looking at our experience, listening to our friends, reflecting on the received ideas we all took in when we were growing up, it seems that many of us are convinced that caring is a limited resource, like a fossil fuel. In this view, caring powers our actions the way gas powers a car. If we try to do too many things, we need to refuel: we only have so much caring. And if we push too hard, we will run out.

We also seem to believe that caring for something means we fail to care for something else, as if we had only a small watering-can and had to decide which of several plants would receive nourishment.

In this view, caring is a question of singling things out and paying attention *to* them.

This pointing to an object probably seems normal—even essential to caring. After all, what is the point of caring, if there is nothing to care about? But it has some surprising consequences for our *capacity* to care. If we are pointing to one thing, it seems impossible to point to anything else. This way of thinking about caring makes caring intrinsically limited.

At the heart of caring is an 'and,' not an 'or.' Deep within us lies a potential that transcends our artificial limitations. Can we embrace the possibility that we are fully capable of caring globally, in every direction—that the compass of our caring could open 360 degrees?

Beliefs that Make Caring Harder

"I have only a limited quantity of caring. If I care for you, I can't care for myself, and vice-versa."

"Hard work and peaceful ease are mutually exclusive. I can do one after the other, but I can't do them both at the same time."

"Caring is the same as worrying; or if they are different, you still need to worry in order to really care."

"Caring is unpleasant; it means doing dirty, thankless jobs."

"My caring generally goes unappreciated."

"Caring is a 'should.' It is motivated by my feeling that I *ought* to care. If I don't care enough, I feel guilty."

"Caring leads to burn-out."

Beliefs that Make Caring Easier

"Maybe I can't solve all the problems, but I can help the person or situation in front of me."

"Caring doesn't need to be showy or superhuman."

"Caring for myself doesn't have to take away from my caring for you."

"Even if people don't always notice, caring makes a difference."

"The energy for caring is always present."

"The more I care, the more I am able to care."

"The heart of caring is appreciation."

Beyond Caring 'About'

We care *about* things; animals, projects, or money. We care about our jobs, about the environment, about the political situation. It's familiar and ordinary, this 'caring about.'

In earlier times, 'about' meant something closer to 'circling around.' That older sense of the word may still be subtly attached to its meaning today: to care about something often seems to mean that my caring goes around the thing I care for, coming to it from the outside.

> *Somehow, this kind of caring feels like me just standing there, watching and worrying helplessly. It doesn't feel very good.*
>
> *Is there another way?*

We need a broader, deeper kind of care. Caring could have a quality almost approaching bliss—the joy of boundless compassion that is free to act, to offer love. If real caring is there, life feels good. We treasure the company of people we love; we take pleasure in simple activities like eating, walking, or just sitting in the sunlight. When we care, we discover beauty in what we perceive.

Caring that has depth—the depth we recognize when we think back on those who have truly cared for us—doesn't just orbit around what it loves. It doesn't just stand there: it goes straight to the heart.

The Quality of Caring

Deep inside all of our cares and concerns there is a quality of caring.

Sometimes it is almost invisible, crowded in by worry or resentment, or covered over by exhaustion. But it persists beneath all this, and while it may not always be easy to contact, it has the power to nourish us.

Those whose thoughts are truly kind don't need to speak: we *feel* their gentleness and desire to help. Being around them makes the heart lighter. Seeing through their eyes, we catch a glimpse of our own goodness and value.

This caring quality is not restricted to any 'from' and 'to' dynamic; instead it enfolds the giver and the recipient in an atmosphere that soothes and heals, almost without our realizing it.

Leaving a hot, arid environment for a cool, temperate one, we can sense a change in the way the air feels in our lungs. We take in healing moisture. Deep inside, we give a sigh of relief: we relax. *That's better,* we think.

The quality of caring is something like this—and when we practice caring, we make its benefits available for everyone. Perhaps we have only ever experienced this kind of care in a limited way, but that doesn't necessarily mean that those limits are built into caring.

Can we touch that fundamental caring directly? When we learn how to recognize it, when we develop our awareness of it, we give it a chance to grow.

Broader and broader it expands: caring soaks into the environment and emerges in beautiful new forms of life. Eventually, the care, the one caring, and the recipient of care all open up, revealing a caring that embraces everything, that ignores and rejects nothing, a luminous *caring mind: caring in all ways, in and through itself.*

Honoring the spirit of this quality of caring, we can make friends with our own minds, our senses, our feelings, our intelligence.

Feeling guilty or inadequate, blaming and shaming ourselves: we can tell there's no caring quality in these things. If there is no caring there, perhaps we shouldn't cultivate these expressions—caring would be so much better all around.

The quality of caring: maybe this is the medicine we so urgently need.

Exercise: The Kindness of Neutral Noticing

How quick we are to judge ourselves! "That was the wrong thing to say, the wrong way to act," we tell ourselves. "I made a mistake." But if we want to understand ourselves—and learn from our mistakes—a gentle, neutral attention to our feelings and thoughts could help us more.

Begin by noticing how often you call yourself an unkind name, or lecture yourself about your behavior. But take care. When we see these things, it's natural to want to respond, to instruct ourselves... even scold ourselves.

"See there! You were mean to yourself again! Stop being so foolish."

Oh... I thought I was just noticing, but even that 'noticing' was kind of mean. How do I stop this?

Noticing doesn't have to involve telling ourselves things; noticing can be gentle, embracing,
and silent. But if you feel like you need to say
something about it all, try saying, *Ah.*

*Ah: there it is. Ah: yes, that's how I behaved. Ah:
that's why I felt those things.*

Let your "ah's" open up, as neutral awareness
deepens into acceptance and understanding.

A Longer View

So much of what we experience pushes us to focus on
ourselves, and to care only about what is happening *right
now.* Burdened by stress, work, family and finances,
preoccupied by the constant cycling of the news, we
may feel pressured to concentrate on security or simply
survival.

Anxiety makes this pressure even harder to tolerate,
driving us to escape into fantasies or trapping us in
painful, obsessive thoughts. These dream-worlds can
sometimes entertain or distract us, but they rarely give
us much in return. The 'tomorrow' they show us is
imaginary, not really connected to our future, or to the
real and awe-inspiring shape of our lives as we move
through time.

Could we develop a broader horizon?

It can be beneficial to imagine our world from the vantage point of a hundred years from now. What do you think will be here? Can we accomplish anything that could endure for that long? Can we act according to such a wide-angle view, live our lives in accordance with such an extensive plan?

This may seem like an unusual idea; not many of us have been brought up to imagine what the world will be like after we have left it. But if we are unable to develop the ability to patiently stick to long-range plans, we lose important opportunities.

Bit by bit, our precious life energy will be lost, and there will be little left to show for our time on earth. The generations that come after us—who could be in even more trouble than we are—will not receive any inheritance, any legacy of wisdom or kindness; and our own dreams will go unrealized. And we will disappear, having helped no one, not even ourselves.

We can see this going on all around us. It's a fate that befalls far too many of us—sometimes people very close to us.

It is a sad story, this empty journey.

Exercise: Protect Your Potentials

Take a moment to reflect on the people in your life who, one way or another, could not achieve their full potential. Consider what their lives might have been like if they had been able to commit to their best selves and bring them into being. Imagine the beauty and goodness they would have added to the world.

Now, make a list of your own inner aspirations, your dreams for yourself. Look at them carefully, and consider whether they are worth a deep investment of your time and energy. If you are convinced, make yourself a promise: in the memory of all your friends and loved ones who couldn't make their aspirations come true, you will do better: you will not give up on yourself.

To develop care, we must make it a mission that we share with one another. You and I, and everyone we know, can encourage one other to care, so that care remains what it has always been—a fundamental in the universe.

This is not simply a pious wish. We should be ready to explore how to bring caring into the heart of science, religion, medicine, and all the other fields in which knowledge now finds expression.

There are countless fields of inquiry in which care can play a role. We can ask about the best diet to support the health of those we care about. We can find ways to sustain the precious resources of our beautiful and nourishing planet. We can consider the consequences of our actions on future generations, carefully investigating how not to cause harm or undermine our own capacity to survive and flourish in the centuries and millennia to come.

If we can pay attention in this way, all our thoughts become caring: knowledge becomes *caring knowledge.*

Exercise: Blooming flower

In this exercise, write a love letter to the present moment. Study it carefully, appreciate its specific details. Tell it how much it matters to you. If the present moment is sad or difficult, treat it as you would a struggling friend; send it encouragement and inspiration.

Developing Stronger Caring

If we lose the ability to care, it becomes easy to act for selfish reasons. That approach, however, only makes us needy. It encourages addiction and conflict, and it almost forces us to turn a blind eye to the consequences of our actions.

In part this may have to do with willful ignorance. A diabetic, for instance, knowing that sugar can cause grave harm to his body, may choose to eat sugar anyway, and pretend that doing so will not affect him. In part, however, the blindness of not caring comes about because we focus so strongly on our own needs that we lose sight of what is going on around us. We can see this tendency expressed in political movements that divide us in order to manipulate us. We can see it when we redefine a situation to make a problem disappear from view.

What would it be like if everyone truly cared—and if our caring led us to develop a knowingness that allowed us to see clearly in all directions and weigh the impact of every action? We cannot say for certain, but we can imagine.

For one, there would be no wars and no territorial conflicts, for we would care for one another without regard to the artificial boundaries that history, aggression, and greed have imposed on a unified world. We could live in harmony, doing what was necessary for the well-being of all.

How strange that we resist this kind of care, and yet how sadly predictable. Wanting to follow 'my' way, seeking only 'my' benefit, we ignore what our actions do to others. We look past the pain and suffering of countless animals raised under horrifying conditions to provide us with food that we do not need to survive. We pay little attention to the suffering of people in other parts of the world, except perhaps when images of suffering force us to confront what is happening. If other people's actions do not affect us directly, we do not concern ourselves much with what they are doing to their enemies, real or imagined.

Of course, we may condemn those who harm others as wrongdoers, we may say that they are confused or misguided; we may wonder at their mistaken ways of thinking and their distorted ways of feeling. Yet, all that does no good if we do not act. In fact, it may cause more harm, for now the 'wrongdoers' join the long lists of those about whose welfare we do not care. When we reject, push away, and refuse to associate, for whatever reason, we are not acting in ways that will restore care to the world.

Each of us must ask how we can best care for this planet, this fragile world on which we live. We must pay attention with an open heart to what is happening in our world, the directions in which this culture is headed, and the harm we are doing or may yet do.

How can we act in the direction of goodness, rightness, and virtue? How can we do what has value? If we do not care for sentient beings, for the environment, and for ourselves, can we truly say that our time on this earth has purpose? If we do not care, if we have no goals toward which we dedicate ourselves, what is the purpose of our being alive?

Fortunately, we do have a guide to better conduct. When our actions consistently produce good results, that is a sign that we have been able to manifest care. When the positive expands and we participate joyfully in its flowering, that is a sign that we are going in a good direction.

A Caring View

Excellence in thought and vastness of vision depend on learning how to care. When we care, we learn how to plan, prevent, prepare, protect, and expand the field of goodness. We learn how to preserve the treasures we have been given.

By caring, we can promote knowledge and transcend the concerns of the self. First we can embody care ourselves, and then we can expand its presence everywhere. That is our duty. It is not a burden, for care begins with care for ourselves: our health, our energy, the conditions we experience, the friendships we enjoy, and the mental environment we depend on. Care leads us to evaluate the products we put in our body and be mindful of the condition of our blood, our cells, our muscles, and our inner organs.

Western science has learned so much. Biology, chemistry, and neurology can teach us in incredible detail what is harmful and what is helpful, even if the knowledge remains provisional and the guidelines they offer change over time. Care counsels us to follow their recommendations unless other forms of knowledge point us in a different direction. But we can also look more widely.

When we care, we ask what is good for the heart and head, the mind and body. We look to the welfare of the self and others: our family, our friends, our community; humanity, the natural world, and all sentient beings. We may not want to look; we may feel shy or afraid to take responsibility. Let care grow within us, however, and we will learn how to look fearlessly, ready to act.

Each of us knows that one day, perhaps soon, our time on earth will be at an end, and our body will disappear. Now is the time to act, to seize every minute, every opportunity, day after day. At home, at work, at play: it does not matter. What matters is care.

When we understand for ourselves the importance of care, we need to share what we understand with our friends, with young people—in fact, with everyone. We can teach, but we can also show by example. Care opens the door to love, respect, appreciation, and a meaningful life. That is the message we can share.

It is easy enough to find examples in the world of people who do not care—perhaps out of ignorance, perhaps out of fear, perhaps through a failure to recognize what is possible. "It's too much," we hear people say; "I don't know what to do to make a difference." But that is the wrong way to look. Right now we can encourage ourselves and encourage others. When we strengthen care, we only make ourselves stronger.

Faith in Caring

If we do not trust our own capacities to cultivate care, we can find inspiration in the remarkable human beings whose traces we find in our histories. The Bodhisattvas of Buddhist tradition manifested care, as did Jesus and other great spiritual leaders. We may not be certain that the stories told by religion are true, but if we even suspect that they are pointing toward a life based on caring, that may be enough. We can dedicate ourselves to a similar goal, following in their example as best we can, for the sake of all sentient beings.

One of the great values of religious traditions is that they think about this question of care. They ask what the mission or purpose of humanity may be. It is not only the religious who think this way, however. We can find inspiration in many places.

This is not a matter of following a particular sect or school or religious tradition. It does not depend on accepting any dogma or sets of beliefs or arguments. These are values that are shared universally, and care is the key to enacting them.

Care brings joy, and once we connect with it, little effort is required. Just pay attention. There may be problems you have been ignoring: now you can act. Keep yourself healthy and productive; renew your body, mind, and spirit; and every day, morning and night, renew your commitment. Study, observe, and open your heart. Share what you know has value, and devise rules and roles that can help you bring the good into being. True happiness requires nothing more.

Without knowing ourselves, all we can offer to others, or to the goals we value, is lip service. Our actions will not be effective if we do not know how to care.

First, therefore, we must encourage ourselves to have faith in and invite caring. We must apply self-caring. That is our homework. Then we can relate this caring beyond ourselves and extend it in ever-widening circles to our community.

Caring Is

Caring is in how we manifest, how we talk, gesture, and act. In that sense, caring is not just another goal: it is a way of being embodied.

Caring means paying attention. We need to understand the conditions, the chemical structures, and the nature of the pros and cons in our experience. When we know what we are doing, we will not make as many mistakes. With caring, we will not later regret our actions.

We do not intentionally set up most of our problems, but they happen anyway. We need a caring hug from ourselves, so that we can communicate directly with our anger, fears, and resentments—so that we have no more separation. By embracing ourselves, we can transform our negativity.

> *In caring, I have a duty; I must first do this now, myself. I will live my life with no regrets. The rest of my life will be my investment in which mind, voice, and activity are inseparable and completely open.*

> *I need to carry on "caring on"—not only once, or sometimes, but constantly caring.*

> *Let this be my secret vow.*

Caring for Ourselves

The nectar of caring is available to us—
and through us, to others.

Depths of Caring

We may hear about compassionate ideals from religion
and wisdom traditions, but before these can be truly
understood, we need to cultivate caring on a personal, immediate level. Caring qualities can develop into
compassion, but if we start with these big words, it is
too easy to miss the present-ness of caring. Loneliness
and confusion result from not knowing how to care on
this fundamental level.

To touch the quality of caring, we will need to go into
the depths of caring. But how are we to do that? How
do we learn to practice better and better caring?

We can all think of things that need more or better care in our lives. We might be able to come up with ideas or methods to help us offer better care. But there is an even more important question when it comes to caring.

How should we care for our own minds?

What should we do about our painful thoughts—our impulsive angers, habit-bound patterns, or distracting, depressing reflections? Those destructive, alienated thoughts can come out of nowhere, cutting in to cause us pain.

It's almost as if an unseen spirit haunts us, ready at any moment to turn our own minds against us. When this spirit is interfering, we can't accomplish much. Meanwhile, without our noticing, our happiness slips away.

If there is an art or skill to living without hurting ourselves, we seem to have lost it.

At an enormous, cultural scale, we seem to have become dependent on things that can lessen our pain temporarily, filling the anxious spaces with food, shopping, books and shows, or contact with friends. But even good friends can't necessarily help us deep inside; close as they may be, they cannot hear our thoughts or experience our dreams with us.

Ultimately, we are the only ones inside our own heads, where ideas, sense-impressions, perceptions, memories, dreams and aspirations are our only company.

It takes a lot of work to maintain good relationships with family and friends. But what about this fundamental companionship?

> *At the very least, at the most basic level of experience, it would be so good to be able to say, in all honesty, "I am happy, I am OK."*

Caring for Mind

Everyone has problems. We experience stress and anxiety, tension, loneliness, agitation, sadness, paranoia, and much more. There are times we feel overwhelmed, when our situation seems hopeless.

Each branch of human understanding, from psychology to philosophy to religion to science to medicine, offers ways to work with such problems. Depending on where we go for help, we may be told to pray or meditate, be given medication to take, or get instructed in ways to analyze our situation differently. Sometimes such measures will prove helpful; other times they will not.

At a more basic level, however, they do not go deep enough. For the source of our problems is the way we have learned to work with mind.

Mind is an incredibly powerful force in our lives, for mind provides the labels we use to make sense of our situation and choose our responses. Its echoes sound in the canyons of our experience. Mind *establishes*, and we shape our encounters with the world through the feed-back that mind makes available. It operates in every waking moment, throughout our lives; perhaps it will even operate in future lives.

Although we can marvel at the rich and varied creations of mind, it would be strange to be completely satisfied with mind's productions. Following the patterns that mind puts in place, we sometimes act in ways that are virtuous and beneficial, but more often we submit to grasping and attachment, ignorance and emotionality.

Is this really what we want? If mind is our servant, is it serving us well?

When we try to understand mind, we quickly run into difficulties. Who gave mind its name and identity? What is the history of mind's arising? What is mind's relation to the nervous system and brain? What is the relation of conscious mind to unconscious mind? The mind is invisible and intangible; we cannot pin it down. We cannot find mind when we look for it, or say what color or shape it has, or even define exactly what it is.

The fact that mind remains a mystery is not surprising, for mind is something of a double agent. When we want to question mind, we investigate with mind, using the labels that mind has provided. When we identify ourselves as the subject perceiving an object, it is mind that gives us these categories. When we are angry or disillusioned, when we agree or disagree with the judgments of others, when we blame or admire, we are feeding back to mind the patterns that mind makes available.

Today there is much talk about how we will soon be able to program robots to serve our needs. Perhaps we could find ways to program or reprogram mind in the same way. If we cannot, we might question whether we ourselves are not the robots, running the programs that mind sets in place.

Could we train mind to function differently? Perhaps we can teach it to care. Perhaps mind can be our partner as we unfold the power of caring. First, however, we must create a caring atmosphere—within the mind and for the mind.

It is not that hard, for caring does not depend on a sophisticated analysis or understanding. What matters is sympathy and sincerity. As we approach mind, we can be honest, straightforward, and kind. "I care," we can say. "I am ready to listen. You have my support. What can I do?"

Ready to care, we can accept whatever happens, saying yes to each new experience and inviting mind to participate in it.

Open to Caring

Caring opens up the closed and defensive reactions the mind has learned to fall into. When mind feels vulnerable, negative thoughts steal in and kidnap our awareness. Past negative patterns re-emerge. If we do not respond with care—calmly and clearly—we will find ourselves carried away, as though a tornado had roared through the middle of our house.

Seeing where negative patterns lead us can help us be aware and attentive. It will do the mind no good to get lost in patterns over which it has no control. When that happens, it is already too late: inner turmoil takes over, and we lose the ability to communicate with ourselves.

In the face of the mind's natural tendency to fall into patterns, we can encourage ourselves to relax, so that we can pay full attention to what is happening. It helps to recognize that the situation we are facing is not unique to us. People everywhere experience the same kinds of frustrations and difficulties. They feel squeezed into tight corners, where any chance at peace has vanished and the natural aliveness of the heart or soul has frozen in place.

We are not the only ones to enter a danger zone, as if we were venturing onto an unstable ice floe, or hiking near a live volcano. We need to recognize the risks: unbearable emotionality, uncontrollable anger, deep despair, icy hatred.

The power of caring can change all this, gentling the internal atmosphere. We start with calm awareness that slows down the mind's operations, creating space for a more open response. In the face of negativity, we can ask simple, basic questions. Where is the negativity now? Are we feeling it in this moment, or are we caught in the grip of a painful memory or the fear of an unknown future? Can we anticipate where these feelings are leading? Can we anticipate the likely consequences for ourselves and others? Can we lightly cultivate a basic awareness?

Can we let caring lead us there?

Viewing the world through the lens of caring is an antidote to the frozen patterns of the mind. Seeing through awareness-eyes, we can recognize what is happening in the present, discern the past history of its arising, and predict the patterns likely to unfold in the future. With this knowledge, we can introduce mind to a new way of acting.

Caring and Appreciation

Our introduction to caring boils down to something very simple:

Whatever we are, whatever we have, we help it improve, body, mind, and spirit. Whatever is good in us, we cultivate. Whatever is green and growing inside ourselves, we appreciate.

Don't be shy about this. It is very important not to ignore who you are, what you have. Difficult as it may be at first, it is possible to learn how to acknowledge yourself. You can even tell yourself, "Yes! I am great. I learned something. I did something. I helped someone. I made a difference."

The more you are able to care about yourself that way, the more your caring will help you to cultivate qualities in yourself you can appreciate. In fact, caring can create a beneficial feedback loop with appreciation.

Exercise: Distraction and Appreciation

When we are tired and frustrated in our daily lives, we become easily distracted. Entertaining ourselves with daydreams, pursuing the imaginary dramas of our favorite streaming shows—or tangling ourselves in the real-life 'drama' of arguments with acquaintances and strangers—may feel good in the short term, but in the end can leave us feeling empty. Worse, these activities rob us of precious, irreplaceable hours of time.

Try this antidote: find one thing to appreciate about what you are doing. You can bring your body and senses into it. You might notice a gentle breeze, a soft carpet under your feet, peaceful surroundings, or the presence of kind people nearby.

Appreciation is especially important when you've completed a challenging task. Make sure you give yourself a little time to celebrate making a deadline, or to admire the way a tended garden or clean floor looks and feels.

If you enjoy this exercise, take it a step further: set aside a moment to appreciate the hard work of others in the same spirit. Focus on specifics, not just bland generalities. Look for positive qualities that are unique to that person's achievement.

Exercise: Being There for Yourself

Any time you feel discouraged, take a moment to sit quietly. Notice your spine, and find the feeling of energy at the center of your body, supporting your head and connecting you to the earth. Steady yourself on it as you would support yourself on a walking stick. Trust it: feel its strength and vitality, and let that feeling expand through your entire body. Appreciate this feeling—as if you are a beautiful young tree, not the biggest yet, maybe, but growing stronger all the time.

Getting the Nectar

I say this so many times, in so many ways, because it is so important:

To bring true caring into the world, we must care for ourselves. We must become skilled in the art of bringing peace and ease to heart and mind.

Many of us have never learned how to make friends with ourselves. The entire idea may simply be foreign. Or we may treat our own company as a poor substitute for true companionship, true pleasure, true enjoyment.

> *How can this self whose faults I know so well be a friend and companion? This body, so often a source of pain? This mind, so far from genuine understanding?*

Our focus tends to be on *things*, whether it's objects we want to own or inner qualities we want to develop. We say to ourselves, "I'd like myself better if I had more admirable aspects. I need to do more, be more: then I'll care for myself."

In the same way that we can't see our own elbow without a mirror, we may not know what it really means to love ourselves without reducing ourselves to objects—things we like or dislike. But this approach—one we may have adopted and lived with since we were children—misses the marvelous beauty of our embodiment.

If we could only notice, only remember how wonderful, how magical our bodies are!

The elegant network of veins and arteries; the awe-inspiring complexity of our nervous systems; the chemistry involved in our brains; the way our bodies' molecules cooperate in order to manifest each of us in our particularity—our bodies ought to fill us with astonishment.

Our embodiment is eminently loveable and deserving of care. When we learn to appreciate this embodiment, we learn to recognize more of our potential, glimpsing opportunities and strengths we didn't realize we had.

When we open our hearts to this marvelous beauty, we stop treating care as something we must earn by being perfect. We feel genuine, intrinsic appreciation for our own being—no strings attached.

When we are able to truly care for ourselves, the channel opens, and we are free to receive the healing and happiness that are our birthright, that are part of our embodiment.

You're the benefactor; you're also the beneficiary. *Opening your heart to yourself is how you open up your capacity to care.*

Opening up that capacity is what generates the quality of care—the healing nectar we so desperately need.

Exercise: Joyful Memories

From the time you wake up in the morning until you go to bed at night, you are making new memories. The kindness with which you treat yourself helps to determine the character of these memories. When we struggle with a lot of painful memories, we can become inhibited from opening up to help and healing in the present moment. On the other hand, when we have very good memories, it is as if we have captured a special essence in our experience. The moment that sparked the memory may have gone, but the feeling remains. That feeling can nourish and support us as we go about our lives. In this way, our memories gradually become a source of strength.

Every night, as you look back over your day, practice letting go of things that bothered you and emphasize the positive things that you remember. It may take some effort to find them at first, so be patient. But even little memories—the sound of a tiny bird, the smell of fresh bread, or the feeling of the sun on your back—can make a difference. They can lend you their beautiful energy.

Exploration: Astonishing Embodiment

Our body is like an enormous continent with countries and regions we may know only by their names. There are the lungs, the heart, kidneys, liver, skin, tissues, bones, to name some organs. Or we classify body differently, into upper, middle, and lower regions, left and right sides, head and throat, inner and outer.

But the body is also vast, like the universe. It is composed of over thirty trillion cells—trillions more cells than there are known galaxies. Each cell contains water that transports oxygen and waste, and aids chemical reactions; science textbooks tell us that we are 65% water. Like the galaxies with which we share substance and origin, we know little of the complex workings of this continent. We have no awareness of the constant movement, activities and intimate functioning of these structures.

We think we own the body, but we have no conscious control over processes like digestion, the enzymes that catalyze chemical reactions, or the replacement of damaged cells. And while the indigenous inhabitants of the body such as muscles, nerves, fat, liver, skin all have different functions, due to their specialization, body systems also depend on one another. For instance, the respiratory system supplies oxygen to digestive, reproductive, skeletal systems (among others), while the respiratory and other systems require both nutrients and ways to remove metabolic wastes. Roles also cross over: the mouth, for example, is a citizen that serves both the respiratory and digestive systems, and the cardiovascular system that brings cells oxygen and nutrients also helps maintain temperature.

Many trillions of our cells—about half of all the cells in the body—are not 'us' at all, but bacteria that live predominantly in the microbiome—the gut—that is so important to digestion and immunity. So who are actually the indigenous inhabitants of the body continent?

Most cells have a nucleus, and all are directed by DNA. While DNA is too small to be viewed by the naked eye, we can well imagine the DNA connection active in each structure and muscle, in circulating blood and catalyzing enzymes. Yet we are not aware of the internal structures that keep us alive any more than we are aware of the turning of the galaxies in space. The enzymes, the nervous system, and the organs work in coordination, and depend on the delicate balancing of many interdependent functions.

From eating to digestion, from breathing to the beating of the heart, the complex interactions that make blood flow and bring nourishment to the cells of the body occur without our conscious effort or awareness.

Our body continents are filled with constant motion. At the microscopic level, after all, there is no sleep, no pausing of the activity that keeps us alive. There might be a 'from' and a 'to' in this motion; yet we are not aware of these interrelated and self-moving systems of biological elements.

Instead, we see continuity of form. We register slow change. We notice once a year at Thanksgiving that someone's hair has gone grey and that more wrinkles have appeared. We grow taller, gain bulk, then lose height and mass when we get old. But underneath these gross changes are constantly shifting rhythms of chemical alterations.

All the parts are moving and transitory; there is never any definitive identity. There is no pause, no rest to the movement of energy in the body, the chemical interactions, the breath, the blood.

We have a duty and opportunity to take care of these wonderful bodies. But when we do not have good knowledge, we do not treat ourselves well. We need to consider how to care for the body, and how to balance and protect body and mind.

After all, mind may be the path-finder, the leader of our journey; but our embodiment is our vehicle.

Sense Potential

Caring more directly for our embodiment could encourage us to take our sensing more seriously.

The beauty of the bodily senses is in how they connect

and interact. In the Tibetan Buddhist tradition, we count six sense organs, not five: for we include the mind. We can visualize each of these organs—eye, ear, nose, tongue, body and mind— as gates that open outward to the world around us, as well as attuning within. Always working, they have different roles to play, each with its specific sense faculty, character and field of operation.

There is a seemingly instant 'call of duty' in the sensing process. We hear, see, and feel almost automatically. Perhaps we should have a different word for what is taken to be bare recognition other than the term 'perception,' because what arises seems to come before any active perceiving, as if it were a chemical function or a prompting of the organs of perception. This process seems to have a mental component as well. We could almost call it a consciousness, except that it seems to be activated before our full awareness of the event of sensing.

It seems there's something prior to the grasping of perception, recognition, naming, and labeling. Although there is not yet an application of the rule of language, or of identification, those activities will follow from this stage, for they are made possible by it.

The senses interact with various systems as they receive stimuli transmitted from the nerves. Subtle processes convey this information to our organs. All the systems are vitalized by the breath, and mind cognizes, identifies, and interprets. Each of these systems has its own pattern and movement, yet somehow what we sense is presented as one integrated experience.

Under normal circumstances, we are oblivious to these patterns and their momentum. But we might receive great benefit from tracing the senses' connections to bodily systems. When we pay attention at this level, we unlock new potentials for our experience. Some of our sense-perceptions might even be entirely transformed by new awareness.

Bringing Care to Our Experience

If we are fortunate, we travel with our ever-changing bodies into old age. In the process, we accomplish some but not all our goals, and inevitably lose family and friends along the way.

> *But that's only human. Life is an unpredictable journey, and all we can hope for is to have more ups than downs.*

But why must we be satisfied with only a little bit of happiness? Perhaps we do not need to be trapped in a poverty of mind that accepts and locks into whatever immediately appears.

It's worth looking more closely at the mechanisms of experience, to see if we can learn what triggers the grasping quality in our perceptions. This may be a little challenging, especially at first. It seems that by the time we become aware, perception already has brought with it associations, discrimination, judging, meaning, interpretation.

But before perception kicks in, the sense organs are open and available. Then *something* appears, like a flash of light, and it finds its way into the causal pathways of the appropriate sense organ.

When recognition happens, a subtle identity is established, and we head into the familiar territory of conceptuality. We get caught in the feedback loops and activity of *minding*. Instantly, we are caught up in likes and dislikes, in pros and cons. We are 'in position.'

Our usual understanding of reality is based on the 'rules' built into perception. Ordinary conceptual mind operates in terms of causes and conditions. This mind makes distinctions and moves in this or that direction.

This is a regime that reinforces positioning and uses perception to enforce the tangible and graspable: with perception, we grab and identify immediately, make the label, and pronounce.

We could think of all these activities as stages on an assembly-line; perceptions are being *manufactured* by sense-activity in the same way that factories produce car parts for vehicles. Thanks to the efficiency of sensing and perception, the 'vehicles' of our experience are ready right away—appearing so smoothly that we may never notice the steps involved in the production process.

With our senses turned on, we drive our vehicles. The vehicle is always ready to function, and each sense is part of this well-oiled machinery.

Is it possible to make changes in this system? What would it take to engage sensing and perception in a truly different way?

Resting within the quality of caring could help cool these processes down, calming our rapid-fire judgments and identifications and giving us a chance to relate differently to the signals our senses engage. Could we learn to be less committed to appearance as it arises, and not so quickly caught up by whatever our senses show? Perhaps we could explore the shimmering or stirring receptive quality that is present before perceptions crystallize. There, we might find open space in which caring could truly blossom.

Space for Caring

Deep within the mysterious operations of our senses, deep in the interplay of perception and memory, there may be marvelous resources we rarely touch.

Just as we can be supported by our own positive thoughts and good memories, we can unlock a basic, deeply nourishing happiness in the operations of our senses.

The key is not to grasp at our experience. Instead, let the *inner space* within the feeling, perception, or memory expand.

This expansion we can practice is not daydreaming; we are not trying to linger somewhere pleasant in our minds or stave off painful thoughts and feelings by clinging to something that feels good. The happiness we seek will not be found in our judgments on our experience.

Instead, explore within. Let your awareness move toward ever-more-open space.

Feel for the space that lets your lungs inflate; feel for the space within and between your cells. Imagine this space is *vast*: space in your bones, space in your organs, space cradling the miraculous operations of your nervous system.

There is space, too, between and within thoughts, between and within all that we sense, perceive, recognize, identify, discern. All the structures of all our knowing appear in and through space.

The macro and micro have this in common—the space between cells and stars. When we contact this space directly, it changes how we relate to the shapes and forms of our experience—the things we long for, the things we fear, the things we just know, for certain, exist.

As space expands, we open indefinitely; how far might this knowing and sensing—this caring—extend?

Embracing the Challenge

Caring awareness allows us to study, in depth and great detail, how the rhythms of our experience occur.

With its help, we can look more closely than we ever have before at the sharp points and hard edges of our value judgments and assumptions. We can learn, by contacting the quality of caring, how to smooth out the ripples, and calm the rough seas of thought and feeling.

The quality of caring pervades every part of experience, showing us how it might be embraced, allowing us to connect with our fellow human beings and the world around us without discriminating, without comparisons.

This approach might even let us revisit our beliefs about the various qualities of our experience. Could every single point along our journey have something truly valuable to offer? If we can embrace them caringly, they might be transformed.

To challenge the stories we have learned to believe about ourselves—to trust and open our hearts to experience, even if it seems scary at first—that takes true caring.

Exercise: A Little Bell

While only a few of us have had the experience of literally being at the beck and call of a ringing bell, many of us use phones and email and have had our concentration disrupted by the 'ping' of an arriving call or message.

This little sound can be anxiety-inducing if we are expecting a tough or tricky communication from someone.

The next time a bell rings or a phone sounds, summoning you, notice the way the sound of the bell creates ripples in your awareness. The shock of the sound might spur you to immediate action; if you are thrown enough off your balance, it can profoundly affect how you respond to this call.

Instead, try this as a practice: When the bell rings, whether it's the phone, the bell that summons you to work, or the sound of email arriving, remain still for long enough to take two or three cool, calm breaths before you respond.

Exploration: Developing Discipline

We often talk about the importance and value of discipline. We may admire discipline in others or chastise ourselves when we discover it lacking within. But we do not often consider how, step by step, to develop discipline.

One way to understand discipline is that it means, on a basic level, *cherishing your priorities.*

In the end, discipline that fosters well-being is not necessarily a matter of control, but of caring.

The Importance of the Goal

We don't just develop discipline for its own sake, but because there are things we would like to do.

To try: Make a list of things you really, truly wish to accomplish in your life, in the short term or the long term. For example:

- cultivate a beautiful garden
- communicate better with loved ones
- develop healthier habits
- learn a new language
- create a work of art
- maintain a regular meditation practice
- deeply understand myself and others

Your list may look very different. What matters is that you care about the things that appear on it.

The Importance of Awareness

Awareness is a great ally of discipline. It lets us notice when we're about to lose our focus; it helps us recognize what pulls us away from our goals. If we discover that we are neglecting ourselves, it helps us to identify needs that are not being met. Awareness can also allow us to recognize when we need help from others.

Treasure your awareness; take care of it by listening to what it has to tell you.

To try: Keep a 'goals' journal; use it to take clear, deliberate note of what's going on in your mind as you care for your long-term goals, and to mark what you are learning about yourself.

The Importance of Patience

Discipline takes time to grow; the tree may not bear fruit right away. When we do not see the changes we were hoping for; when a task is harder than we expected; when we struggle with the consequences of poor planning or decision-making—this is when we most need to cultivate patience.

The goal may seem distant; our concentration may flicker in and out.

But if we are convinced of the value and meaningfulness of our goals, if we have faith in the path we take to reach them, then we can patiently put one foot in front of the other. Sometimes, only patience is what lets us win through.

To try: Before you get down to work on a project or task, spend a few moments visualizing it in all its beauty and positive potential. Whether you are scrubbing a bathroom, training for a marathon, writing a book, or looking after a relative who is ill, take time at the start to pour positive energy into what you care about. Reaffirm your commitment to caring.

The Importance of Self-Encouragement

Listen carefully to how you talk to yourself. Ask yourself honestly if you treat yourself well. Would you condone the words you throw at yourself if they were aimed at an animal or a child?

As children, we are more likely to prosper when we receive kindly encouragement from our parents, teachers, and friends. As adults, we can be our own kindly guide and companion.

For self-encouragement to succeed, it must be consistent and genuine. Imagine you work at a call center that handles emergency calls from people who have been in auto accidents. Your voice on the line is there to help keep the person calm and awake—you are there to help them help themselves.

We can treat ourselves in exactly the same way. Even if we seem undisturbed on the surface, we know in our hearts that we are in urgent need of kind, calm, practical encouragement.

To try: Actively change your script. When you hear discouraging, denigrating internal voices, offer yourself a new set of lines to read. Tell yourself: "In the past, I put you down. Now, I want to help you succeed."

The Importance of Ease

At first, ease seems like the opposite of discipline. After all, what does resting or relaxing have to do with achieving our goals? But ease creates the cushion that makes it possible to work harder for what we love and value. It provides inner refreshment that allows us to offer more of ourselves. We achieve more when we are truly relaxed; when we add concentration to ease, great, troubling clouds may disperse.

To try: Take a timed break. No matter how pressed for time you are during your normal day, see if you can put aside a few specific moments to relax. Stretch your body; drink some water; rest your eyes. These small breaks, sprinkled throughout the day, can actually improve productivity and help you avoid burning out.

The Importance of Trusting Yourself

You may find several other factors that are important to you for the development of your discipline. Notice what supports you most as you pursue your goals. Could others benefit from what you have learned?

The Ripple's Ocean Journey

Whether or not we have a good life journey is very dependent on how the mind understands what's going on. Every aspect of our experience—from how we taste the food we eat to the way we absorb the air we breathe—is connected to the activities of our minds. We have far more power to make our journey a good one than we realize.

We often take a 'tourist' approach to experience. Some people can go on remarkable journeys—real adventures—and nevertheless get very little out of what they see, feel and do. But this life of ours—this big journey we are on—is very important, far more significant than a single vacation.

Every day brings a different quality in experience; nothing stays the same, whether it's the environment, the people we are with, the seasons, the politics, or just the weather.

If we are really going to fully express care, for ourselves and others, then we need to learn how to navigate the disturbing alterations, the emotional intensities, and the physical and mental challenges that will inevitably come along.

How do we work with the sharp edge of a short temper, the cold shock of an unexpected deadline?

Perhaps there's a way to get something positive out of this apparent obstacle.

When waves roll through the ocean, the water is not harmed. The variations arise and pass away; all the time, the ocean remains the ocean.

Similarly, the varied characters of our experiences—the vivid happenings that make up our journey—are mind's own ripples, its own magical variations, born of the subtle interplay of time and space and its power to find patterns, to compare and contrast. If we can understand our experience this way, it may change how we feel about what is going on.

If we really recognize that our ups and downs are painful because mind has mistaken its own ripples for real things, then the obstacles to our happiness disappear.

Exercise: The Source of the Squeeze

Presented with a challenge, we have a choice: we can support ourselves, or we can become a burden to ourselves—or even become our own worst enemy.

Think back to a moment when you felt you were under duress. How did you relate to your trouble? More importantly, how did you relate to yourself? Can you trace the role your mind played in creating the stress?

Sometimes, especially at first, obstacles can arise when we try to care for ourselves. Inner and outer stress may intensify when we respond with gentleness. Our thoughts and feelings might get rougher than before. We might even experience external events that seem designed to squash our efforts to take care of ourselves. It's as if the outside world and our own thoughts are conspiring against us. "You think you're tough, do you!" But this aggressiveness masks a lot of insecurity on the part of mind.

Even under normal circumstances, the mind is conditioned to live from crisis to crisis. Even just *trying* to relax can activate that conditioning, causing a backlash of anxiety. Under circumstances our minds identify as crises, it's even worse. It's as if our worries have hold of our hand and they are squeezing hard.

What is the source of the squeeze? If you have *decided* you are afraid; if you have *decided* it is impossible; if you have *decided* you are depressed or exhausted, you will feel the squeeze. But this is a mind trick.

When your worries start to squeeze, when your thoughts start to exert pressure, don't struggle against them—that makes the pressure worse.

Instead, try telling yourself: "I decided I was in trouble; I've really made myself uncomfortable!

I decided this was too much; that's why you're squeezing now. I have many other ways I can experience this, though! It all depends on my view. If my view is powerful enough to make me miserable, maybe it's powerful enough to make me really happy."

Close your eyes, and visualize that you are pure, cool water. This stress seems intense, dominating—but it's just a wave form, passing through. It can't swamp you, because it is you—it is made of your energy, your essence.

The pure, cool water gradually grows still, becoming very clear.

The little wave moves on through, and ripples away.

Sharing Caring

Recognizing the need, learning the methods, opening our own hearts to caring, all lead us to a decision-point: can we take responsibility for sharing caring?

Open to the World

The path of caring is not only for times when we are alone, not only a topic for our meditation. It is open to the world.

Take a moment to think about how many times you interact with others over the course of the day. Recall the casual greetings and brief exchanges, the formal meetings and long conversations. Each point of contact has the potential to be a vehicle of the quality of care we have discovered within.

Even when we do not speak, our body language and gestures can be powerful vehicles—we can reassure others with the touch of a hand. Even our calm, steady breathing can help others feel more at ease.

This quality also manifests when we relate to the larger world with kindness and attention. It is present when we avoid stepping on beetles, when we gently move aside branches or plants that are in our path, and when we open and close doors smoothly and quietly. Everything we do, every movement we make, can be a way to communicate caring.

When people sense your quality of care, they become more positive, more optimistic. It becomes easier for joy to emerge in their daily lives.

Outer, Inner, and Secret Lives

As we consider caring, it is valuable to reflect on those whom we do not care about. We might not like to admit it, but even when we try to be open-minded and agreeable, almost all of us place a few conditions on our caring.

Who counts as uncared-for depends on the ways we ourselves identify with others. Some of us pay no attention to animals or plants. Some of us are considerate of children, but dislike being around the elderly. For some, it's the other way around.

And almost all of us have made a private, personal decision about individuals or groups we do not like.

Some people don't deserve care.

There are people alive today whose beautiful potentials go virtually ignored by the world—because they are homeless, or disabled, or because they come from the 'wrong' country or practice the 'wrong' religion.

On the other hand, we may feel able to reach out a friendly hand to groups that have been traditionally overlooked or abused, but find ourselves unable to care about people we regard as privileged, rich and successful.

> *Why should I care about them? They have it all. More than me!*

This bitterness is pretty common, and quite understandable, given the way we have learned to relate to ourselves. Yet when we care, we realize that all human beings have outer, inner, and secret lives. What we show to others, our outer lives, may bear little resemblance to our inner lives—the world of thoughts and feelings, memories and fears that colors all we do. At an even deeper level are experiences we may not even be able to share consciously with ourselves—our truly secret lives.

It is important to consider this, because those with prosperous outer lives may be suffering unimaginably. A wealthy and famous entertainer, beloved by millions of 'fans,' may be deeply isolated, frightened and ill, even literally starving. That person may never have tasted real joy, or kind, reliable caring.

The outer form, the inner atmosphere, and the secret story may not match.

Beyond Bias

The casual discriminations we practice in our daily lives were not part of us as children. We took our biases on gradually; you could say we were educated into our ignorance.

We can unlearn the biases that keep us separate, let go of these dismissive, defensive behaviors, and learn valuable lessons from those who live miserable inner lives, who suffer from torments the best medical care and the finest food will not ameliorate.

When we cultivate the quality of caring, we taste a flavor that, unfortunately, only a few of us know well. Here too there are many layers. Even if our lives appear lonely from the outside, when we care for ourselves, we have inner resources, inner depths, that sustain us and allow us to give genuine kindness to others. Friends with our own sense of body and mind, we can show others a special spirit. Even if we have very little by way of material goods or comforts, we have the inner support of our own confidence: we know we are OK.

The more deeply we partake of the nectar of caring, the more capable we are of leaving behind our biases and resentments. The more we care for ourselves, the more obvious to us others' need for care becomes.

Starting Small and Simple

We can at least start now on a smaller scale, with an immediate way of caring:

I can only do so much, but I can do this now.

We might start by practicing to develop present-ness and openness. When we are truly present and can feel another's troubles and offer support, we are caring. We can even feel for animals, beings that cannot advocate for themselves in our language-oriented world. Each moment, we can remind ourselves to pay attention to what is happening, and respond to others with kindly, thoughtful communication.

We can do this on an immediate and physical level by taking care of such simple things as cleaning implements and gardening tools. We can pay attention to how we tend flowers and plants, and how we respect animals. We can care for the spaces and neighborhoods where we live. We can care for our bodies and nurture the energies that must flow so that we can accomplish our aims.

In relating with others, we can learn how to create a friendly atmosphere. The impressions we leave and the attitudes we bring influence and can encourage others. We can strengthen our caring by listening and paying attention to the feedback we receive from our actions— by accepting a friend's gratitude for our help, for instance, or by embracing a sense of accomplishment for a job well done.

Careful attention to the feedback we receive from unsuccessful efforts is also important. We can develop a level of caring that does not depend on being rewarded —even if only subtly—for our actions. Then our expressions of care may become more available for anyone in need, even for someone ill in body or spirit, or destitute and homeless.

According to Buddhist tradition, the Bodhisattva manifests a higher level of caring for those who are ignorant. No response or feedback from the recipient of that caring is expected. This is the kind of selfless love and compassion described in the highest religious ideals.

Yet, without everyday caring in mundane matters, this activity may simply be invisible to us. It can be hard to imagine anyone really being or acting like this, and so our minds may translate Bodhisattva activity into something conceptual, idealized, and ultimately abstract.

If compassion and caring register only as words or thoughts, without a living connection to the heart, there is little understanding. Words remain concepts without much effect unless we have developed that heart connection. Ordinary-level, daily caring is crucial for us to develop our understanding of care.

Caring beyond Concepts

We need to develop a 'first grade' level of caring: a basic understanding of how to take advantage of our opportunities and enjoy life.

Too many people have not been taught how to take care of themselves, their bodies, or their thoughts. Americans in general, it seems, thrive on youthful energy, and this can make caring more difficult. The young are always on the go, and they never think about getting old. No one is teaching them how best to make their way to harmony, balance, and joy. They learn the hard way, if at all, through tragedy, fatal mistakes, or searching for happiness in the wrong places.

Those of us who are educators do not seem to be reaching our students on the higher levels of human being—for we ourselves are not reaching those higher levels of selflessness and compassion. We educators need to do more than just tell people that they should do this and not do that. We need to teach in an integrated way to reach that higher level.

We can do that, not by invoking a selfless caring, or by discussing an abstract, ideal Bodhisattva way of compassion, but by focusing on our shared human condition: our assumption of identity, the rule of language and concept, and the way we have fallen under the dictatorship of mind.

This education cannot be an intellectual exercise; caring is not a lecture that we give. It must be modeled, embodied, expressed.

After all, we have been told many, many times to be mindful, to be aware, to be caring, to pay attention. It is important to realize that somebody has been translating for us, all this time: dictating, expressing, and influencing our impressions.

> *And something in me is following this lead as if I am a donkey following a carrot on a string. I don't know where it came from, but I'm hungry. And the carrot-concept looks juicy....*
>
> *However, I have a feeling... I have a feeling there will be no progress if this caring is an abstract idea, an expression only. Until we see through the dictation, caring will not reach the heart.*

There are some positive aspects to training in caring the way a donkey chases a carrot. However flawed our words may be in conveying caring, we need to use language to catch our listener's attention. As teachers, we can dangle carrots in order to initiate the inquiry. It is also important to give encouragement; we may need a little pat on the back to help us learn.

It's true that there is always a danger that the intention of caring, or the expression of caring, is secretly looking for feedback. But that, too, is all right. We learn caring for the self if the feedback from letting go is peace. We learn caring for others if the feedback connects to the heart. Gradually, giving and receiving care form a unity; then, we need not depend so much on feedback.

The Bodhisattva does not need any feedback, for the Bodhisattva responds to ignorance with total compassion. The Bodhisattva sees, *and sees through*, the subject-object orientation, and salutes the shining mind, the empty space at the heart of all shape and form.

In this sense, caring is a direct response to ignorance.

Ways of Caring

Perhaps we, as ordinary humans, cannot communicate at this higher level; but we *can* point the way to self-caring, and share with others the simple joy of being alive. Joy is a clear, straightforward, 'first level' teaching. And this much we can show. We may have limits on our giving, but we can demonstrate a way to take delight in our own embodiment.

An aspiration to care is needed for that communication. We need a good intention and a wish to help others. But then we must turn this intention into accomplishment.

We may recognize that we have only a limited sense of how to do this. But we can respond as best we can to the lack of caring we sense beneath appearances. So many people don't know how to care, how to have joy and to love themselves. Their bodies and minds are so tense, their hearts so daunted, that many of them are growing numb. When we respond with caring, its effects can ripple outward, and bring life and energy to these cold, numb places.

The subtlety of these movements reminds us that we may need to offer caring indirectly. Language provides us limited resources in this regard, for in words, we can express only the past patterns of our experience. These patterns are already set up: concepts and behaviors are already present, and new ones are in production. The wheel goes forward, and we have no choice but to engage.

There is no easy way out; we have to work with what presents itself, and relate to people where they are. On the other hand, without these concepts and beliefs— these manifestations of mind—we couldn't discover a graduated path of understanding, *a way to care.*

We are not talking about perfect realization. These lessons are for our *whole* journey, beginning, middle, and end, not just for when we are all highly advanced. No matter how much we understand now, we want to graduate, to progress, to go forward.

As we develop, as we learn more and more about our ways of caring, our understanding will gradually open up. We can have a wider compass, a greater circumference for our caring. That gives us a kind of inner grace or blessing that we can recognize in our lives.

These ways of caring could be very good vehicles.

Humble Heart

In our efforts to care for others, there may come times when we try our best but fail to accomplish what we hoped, or when we discover we don't yet know how to fully share the quality of caring.

We might be deeply concerned with the suffering of our loved ones, but uncertain how to help. We try to do as much as we can on a human level, but because we still have much to learn about ourselves, we don't yet have the depth that would help us know what to do. In these cases, for thousands of years, human beings have turned to prayer.

Not all of us will feel comfortable with the idea of prayer; if you are not religious, it might be more helpful to meditate on the living possibility of a greater goodness, a greater power for healing. Remember the human beings that seem to you most admirable; keep their example close by.

For those who follow the path of Dharma, the Buddha, the Bodhisattvas and the great beings who have sometimes walked among us possess this depth of understanding we sense is lacking, in the world and in ourselves—which is why Buddhists believe that Bodhisattvas have a great power to transmit blessings.

I know from my own experience that these great masters, these matchless teachers, do care for us sentient beings. If you pray, they do not turn away.

Even though we have personal limits, we can call on the Enlightened Ones. They know we are ignorant and they respond, because their mission is to transform ignorance. And they have deep sympathy and compassion for us—precisely because we are ignorant.

Calling for Aid

If you know you are sick, you need to call doctors and healers. It's the same when you call on the Enlightened Ones: they come directly to respond. They are dedicated to goodness, right action, right virtue. And our ignorance can be cleared away with the blessings that come on our behalf.

When a task is beyond us, we can pray: "I need your help." By invoking prayer, we become agents of the Bodhisattvas, on a mission of caring. The power of blessing comes because of their caring. They tell us: Be aware of caring. Help others. Embody goodness. They remind us: we can care as much as they do.

To embody these virtues for ourselves, we need a way to clear away the residues of our long-standing way of being. Water makes it much easier to get clean; likewise, the quality of caring found in the blessings of these great beings makes it easier to open our hearts to transformation.

Ultimately, our duty is to take on the responsibility of caring. This is not a duty that is forced on us, like the duty to fulfill a social obligation. Rather, it arises naturally as a heartfelt response to suffering. But we may need help to be more caring. Great masters like Padmasambhava have given us tools and methods; with his help, and the help of great exemplars and teachers throughout human history, we can make a serious, committed study of how to serve and help others.

What the Heart Knows

There is an important role for our cognitive minds in the work of caring, because paying attention, noticing, is at the basis of caring.

Therefore, we need to be conscious of our caring, and care carefully. Preparation, and conscious attention on the cognitive level, can spare us much disappointment.

But in caring at a higher level, there is no measurement, no making distinctions. We are not looking to receive feedback; it is not the reason we do it. Rather, we are working because of the situation we are all in.

In the end, conceptual instructions like "Pay attention" are mind's expressions, its thoughts. Even having the intention to care is still an operation of mind. We need more than that: we need heart.

Prayer can open the heart, so that when we are discouraged we do not give up. If we are sincere, asking for guidance—heart to heart—our hearts will communicate an inner message, as will the senses. The heart will lend its power, intelligence, and encouragement to all we do.

We could call this way a secret path, for it is deeply personal, and is not about external shows of religious feeling. We do not seek to convert others to our way of life. We are simply messengers of caring.

Caring Messenger

If you are a messenger for caring, it is up to you to make it manifest. How can you deliver the message? How can you communicate its importance? How can you develop the wisdom and intelligence to share the healing power of care?

You could start by imagining that you are the only one who understands the importance of care. It is as though you somehow found the formula for a medicine that could cure a terrible disease. It is up to you to act! All humanity is waiting, wrapped in despair, hopeless, alone—in utter devastation. But you have the power to do something about it.

Say to yourself, with real conviction, "I care." Let yourself feel strong sympathy and compassion, and you will know what to do. You will naturally take responsibility, the way parents take complete responsibility for their child. As empathy and concern arise, you will find yourself in a realm where blessings and healing flow freely.

Taking care starts with our own mind and feelings, our closest friends and companions. When the mind feels cared for and we are ready to guide our feelings in positive directions, we can relax. No longer as needy, we are ready to take care of others.

Our personal situation may be positive and healthy, but now we see that is not enough. When we ourselves are free of problems, we have a foundation for expanding our vision to include the welfare of others and of the world we inhabit together.

Exploration: Culture of Neglect

When we look at the news, it's hard not to think that our world seems intent on hurting itself. Partisanship and divisiveness dominate cultural expression, creating biases and social discrimination. We seem to care only for the demands of the self—for *my beliefs, my religion, my way, right or wrong.*

Although civil society is intended to improve our lives, insults, harsh words and untruths have become accepted political tools. Many leaders engineer their own profit and consolidate power at the expense of vulnerable constituents; they rarely engage broader issues, or pursue a truly penetrating vision of the future.

We just don't take care of one another.

Those in education, knowledge fields, and communication also seem to inhabit a world lacking in caring.

Doctors understand pain and suffering, but they are obliged by law to keep a professional distance; they often must serve within a bureaucracy that makes it harder to attend with care to their patients' stories and to spend as much time as is needed with them.

It seems all of us are too preoccupied with our own lives to care about anything else, let alone all sentient beings. Yet if we are unable to find ways of caring, we are planting seeds of destruction. There is not much quality or nutrition in all the hustling and rustling in our distracted lives.

We can clearly see the tragic impact of neglect in American society. Credible sources tell us that one in six children in America can't count on regular food. Divorce rates range between forty and fifty percent. Most schools now hold mass shooting drills, with students learning how to lock and barricade their classroom doors against attacks that might come from their own classmates. The needs of the elderly are ignored.

People do not know how to share joy in communicating with each other, and technology has greatly complicated the world. Mobile interactive technologies are racing to turn human attention into financial profit, using algorithms to hook users.

We need to develop a more heartfelt kind of caring, a caring that *counts*—like a mother's love for her only child. We need a virtuous and respectful way of caring. Only then can caring lead to real, effective change in our cultures.

Caring in a World of Hurt

To extend the circle of care outwards, we can start with our friends, our family, and our loved ones. We can be sensitive to the needs of our community, the organizations we participate in, and the people we work with. Most people stop there, for we have learned to accept the truth of the labels we use to separate one group from another, one race from another, one ideology or belief system from another. We may see the harm that befalls our enemies as a victory, but that makes no sense even on the practical level. The suffering of our enemies does nothing to protect us.

The world has known so much conflict through the centuries. One nation invades another, and people with no stake in the outcome are suddenly the victims. What do such battles accomplish? Even if the course of history is changed, people's lives go on as they always have. Conquests and regime changes are recorded in the history books, but in the end, what difference does it make?

Tibet is a good example. The earliest Tibetan records go back some 2,200 years. For many centuries the rulers of Tibet gradually expanded their power, until in the seventh and eighth centuries, under the Dharma kings Srongtsen Gampo and Trisong Detsen, Tibet became a powerful empire, ruling much of Asia. By the middle of the ninth century, however, much of the empire had collapsed. Wars and conflicts and rivalries continued over the next millennium, with one party seizing power and then the other.

Today, none of that matters. Tibet has been absorbed into its more powerful neighbor, and its language and culture are at risk of disappearing. Similar fates have befallen countless countries that once reckoned themselves powerful, even invincible.

Looking at the records of history, we come to see that we all share a common humanity. The ups and downs of one nation or country, one ideology or another, do not alter this fundamental fact. Taking too narrow a view only obscures the truth of suffering and the universal aspirations that all people have for peace and freedom.

America was one of the first countries to realize the importance of freedom and ground itself in that realization. This simple fact in some ways sets America apart. Yet America, too, has acted at many points in its history to undermine the cause of freedom. It has disregarded the rights of other countries and worked to maximize its own power. At times it has served selflessly to safeguard the rights of the poor and the weak, but at other times it has ignored the harm it has caused in the world. Could caring at a deep level have written the historical record differently?

If they are not informed by the power of care, concepts like freedom, truth, and realization can easily become empty names. When we truly care, however—when leaders understand that there is no benefit in harming others—then freedom becomes inseparable from respect and appreciation for the world's diversity. We no longer react on the basis of our own emotions, wants, and needs. Freeing ourselves inwardly, we look outward to see what the world needs, and we act accordingly.

When we place limits on our caring, drawing boundaries that exclude one person, one group, or one kind of being, caring shuts down, and then its power to work in our lives is restricted as well. But when we let caring grow in accord with its own inner momentum, its full power manifests. We naturally find ourselves concerned with all humanity, and beyond that with beings everywhere.

History teaches us that war, famine, disease, and natural disasters are always with us. The tragedies that unfold all around us, sometimes unexpectedly touching our own lives, are a reminder that suffering knows no limits. It is not hard to see that many people today find themselves trapped in the hell realms of suffering.

We cannot expect that care will solve every problem, but if we approach each situation gently, asking what we can do to help, the field of caring and its power to bring benefit will grow and grow. It is a path that opens naturally and with ease.

A Study in Caring

We ordinarily learn from our parents, family, and friends how to express caring in our lives. If we pay attention and reflect on the feedback we receive, we can begin to appreciate its real value.

Our family members may not have been able to express their caring effectively, and may not have been aware of what they were passing on. Perhaps they could not share their knowledge of how to become independent, how to pursue goals, how to develop the qualities that will make us happy and successful.

If that is so, then we must study the art of caring, ourselves: our lives must be our own responsibility. If we can take responsibility for our own caring, we can leave a powerful legacy to those who follow us.

There are very practical lessons in caring we can find each moment, every day. In every situation, there is something to care about. Wherever we go, whatever we do, we can develop our caring by directing attention: *What is the quality of my caring, and what do I see to care about at this very moment? How much energy have I expended in a way I have not done before?*

Any expression, any sensory operation, any communication can be an example and expression of caring.

Gestures of Caring

There are simple, everyday gestures that can communicate our care and our wish to help. A touch, a friendly expression, a smile, or a direct and accepting gaze: these all show that we are available, ready to be of help. In this culture, people shake hands when they meet, and perhaps that shows a certain readiness and openness—a feeling of solidarity. Yet we could take this much further. Can our every action refresh those we meet? Can we practice caring in the morning, the afternoon, and the evening? Can our words be friendly and positive?

Such gestures are small, but they can make a real difference. We can practice them ourselves, and we can also teach them to children, encouraging an attitude of respect and appreciation. Young children seem to know without any formal instruction how to be kind and caring, at least some of the time. But after a certain age, they withdraw into their own isolated worlds. To create a more caring future, we need to support and nurture the caring hearts of young people, so they may carry caring into adulthood.

Imagine the impact if our educational system emphasized caring and the knowledge that supports it. Individuals would have the resources to care for themselves and for one another. Being familiar with their own minds and bodies, people could communicate on the basis of friendship and mutual trust, leading to real dialogue. Their small gestures of caring could transform the arid desert of isolation into the green valleys of joy and mutual respect.

The public world, too, is urgently in need of gestures of caring. Politicians and diplomats learn persuasive gestures and a special language that conceals as much as it reveals, but the rest of us need a different way of communicating, one that reflects the inner truth of our sincere caring. When we live in community with others, we need to pay close attention to their needs. Caring from the inside out, we can commit to service.

To really make a difference, however, we need to overcome the ignorance that comes when we do not care. That is the real enemy. When we do not know the conditions that lead to suffering, we cannot act to overcome it. When we do not recognize the value of care, we miss our opportunity to be of benefit.

That is why growing in knowledge is itself a gesture of caring.

Responsible for Caring

A simple gesture of caring can mean a great deal, and meritorious actions open the door to compassion. The world's religious and spiritual traditions all recognize this truth, and the great leaders they honor have all been guided by it. Buddhism speaks of the Great Bodhisattvas, while other traditions speak of angels, saints, and holy messengers. These remarkable caregivers have been dedicated to alleviating suffering, whether it appears in the form of demons and devils, or is characterized as neuroses, illness, and pain. Their wisdom gives rise to boundless care and compassion.

Because churches, synagogues, temples, and mosques are human institutions, they can be corrupted. At their best, however, they exist to serve and care for their followers and those who come to them in need. No matter what their doctrines, their mission is to offer grace, love, and inner healing. As vehicles for care and compassion, they each maintain their own lineages of caring, which deserve our respect and gratitude.

In many ways, they uphold the principle of taking responsibility for caring; and we can emulate the steadfast commitment to that responsibility that their best exemplars display.

Responsibility for caring manifests in being willing to question our experience. For instance, when tensions arise, we quickly give in to them. Why is that? Why do we accept the truth of their claims? When negative emotions arise, why do we so quickly go along with them? How might we respond differently?

In this kind of inquiry, the starting point is inner calm. There are feelings that bubble to the surface like lava flowing from a volcano, but if we approach them gently, simply being aware of what is happening, we can learn to negotiate with our own inner pronouncements. When an emotion has already bubbled over, it is too late to do much about it, but before that happens, we have more choices, more alternatives. Before the resentment and delusion, the frustration and the negative energy, we can enter into a dialogue with the mind that is producing these kinds of reactions. We can engage the mind differently.

When we sense that negative feelings have started to arise, we can sort through exactly what is going on. Is the mind directly involved? Do thoughts play a role?

How do the emerging feelings relate to consciousness or cognition? It is not enough to identify the specific flavor of negativity: resentment, disillusionment, discomfort, envy, etc. We need to go deeper and respond more immediately.

Before the turmoil of emotionality takes hold, before the full weight of emerging negativity pops into existence and we find ourselves overwhelmed, we need to look with care, calmly searching. Our attitude does not have to be disapproving or defensive. Instead, we can react with sympathy, like a wise counselor ready to offer assistance.

Caring Guidance

In truth, making a difference is not complicated. It is a simple matter of caring for ourselves and caring for the mind. For instance, almost all of us could attest to the way that greater caring would improve our working lives. The harassed, jostled character of the ordinary working day, with its major and minor irritations, is like a constant, low-grade ache, a quiet cry for better care.

What can we bring to this situation? If we have little power to make material changes, what can we improve? Is there any way to reframe what we experience in order to uncover a more positive impact, view, or expression? Perhaps some behavior we notice in ourselves or others is painful or creating stress; can we find a way to get something beneficial out of this manifestation?

With the right approach, the painful behavior could become the vehicle for a useful lesson, a meaningful change of heart, a broadening perspective, a deeper understanding, or a brighter optimism. Many other treasures could be waiting, ready to emerge with help, with a little caring attention.

Good parents are always trying to give their children a positive, confident outlook, guiding and encouraging them with gestures and words. We know how important that kind of communication can be. In a similar way, we can seek to communicate with the people around us with the same kind consideration, no matter their age, background, or situation in life; we can respect them all.

The Buddhist tradition loves the symbol of the lotus, a beautiful flower that grows best in muddy water. Remembering that lesson of transformation, we can strive to bring goodness out in ourselves and others, no matter what the circumstances.

Without this ongoing, caring effort, families fall apart; communities cannot survive. It is especially important to cultivate this spirit of respect, this energetic seeking after the positive qualities of ourselves and others, when we undertake large projects together.

Large projects require cooperation and mutual under-standing. They require caring. For such projects to be truly successful we must care not only for the project itself in its material aspects, but also for the well-being and peace of mind of all who participate.

Exercise: Time for Caring

Whether you work on your own or in a group, you probably have a project or goal of some kind that you care about—whether it's homeschool-ing young children, designing a building, or looking out for your crew on a difficult job.

Try to incorporate moments into each working day in which you take time to reconnect with your goal, support and encourage yourself and your partners or team, and deliberately release your anxieties, worries and grudges. Even twen-ty minutes of peace can make a big difference in our quality of life, and can change the energy of a classroom, a home, or a workplace.

Suffering and ignorance are no theory: they are real.

For that reason, when it comes to caring, we need to remember the practical side as much as possible. We need to practice daily how to take care of thoughts, emotions, and problems. We need to care about the simple, ordinary specifics of how a team works together and not neglect interpersonal tensions.

Watch closely. Plan well in advance, and apply your beliefs in practice. When a project is underway, notice how much time is left, and consider what can be done to meet the goal. Make the best use of your materials and follow through on whatever is good in your work. It really is important to care at this level of detail.

Caring Communication

Eventually, our caring could graduate to a new level; it may become truly selfless. If we care well, if it is deep, free from positions, it may become completely open, and utterly beyond description.

If caring is truly beyond description, what role can language play in the expansion of caring?

It seems that language emulates language, echoing what has gone before. From word to word, concept to concept, the world is mapped out. But mind made conceptual language.

And mind made caring, too.

Looked at differently: without mind, there is no language. Without perception, there are no concepts. We could not cognize. If we can't cognize, we can't identify with 'reality'—the good or the bad. Cognizing mind has a part to play in the unfolding of knowledge, and language is its instrument. In this way, language, too, can be a vehicle for caring.

Sharing caring touches on the mystery of good communication. It touches others through these words, these shapes and forms that are based on nothing but comparisons, distinctions, relationships, and ratios of ratios.

How magical, how strange! How could this occur?

Mind relates to 'things' and presents itself as a subject, a 'someone.' But the agent of its communiqué is not 'someone.' *It is caring itself.* Caring reaches out, and what is communicated is caring.

When caring is the message we convey, the 'thing' we talk about starts to shed its language-imposed limitations. The role of 'speaker' begins to shimmer, making space for something larger than any one soul.

We must do our best to have faith in this extraordinary power of caring to communicate beyond the bounds of reason, habit … even sense-experience.

But this cannot be a blind faith; when we care, we must be careful with words. If the language we use is jarring or unfamiliar, people will reject the message even if it is accurate, or even if the spirit of what we say is kind. We need to use language that respects those with whom we communicate—meeting them right where they are.

If we don't, they may say "I don't get it." "I don't need it." "I don't care."

If I don't get it, if I don't understand, how can I care?

Bridges to Caring

The truly great and enlightened beings our world has known may not have operated according to the expectations of a 'self.' Their awesome example is still with us today in many ways; it is a precious sign of possibilities we are still in the process of discovering.

For now, we ordinary people still live with our 'selves.' We spend our lives within the strict confines provided by 'I,' 'me,' 'mine,' and 'mind.' This structure is somehow needy: it makes constant demands on us that we must satisfy.

> *I need to be liked. I need to be entertained. I need that thing; please give it to me. I need answers for my peace of mind!*

But these frustrating limitations can also become touch-points for beautiful new ways of life. Having been born in a human body, you have the potential to transform your limitations into bridges across the alienating gulfs that lie between the beings on this planet. 'I' 'me,' 'mine' and 'mind' can become vehicles that let you reach and help others.

We have the ability to transform each and every thought, feeling, and sense-perception into a treasure—so that even when we are alone, even if the world would characterize us as poor in material goods, and no matter where we are, we can enjoy our lives.

This joy becomes care, the basis of our willingness to help others.

Exploration: How to Create a More Caring World

These reflections, written by Tsering Gellek, director of the Sarnath International Nyingma Institute, encourage us to open our hearts to the subtle and blatant forms of suffering that surround us— for it is only when we have allowed ourselves to recognize that pain that we can look for lasting and meaningful healing.

To care is to really understand that we are in a very concerning situation.

As the individual in modern society moves through various spheres of life, from home, to school, to work, to perhaps hospitals and eventually death, she often has less and less support from the people around her. When I imagine earlier times, I think there was a deeper sense of care from family, friends and neighbors, from our religious or sacred communities, from the towns and villages we lived in. This atmosphere of care, of *embeddedness*, of being interwoven into a larger fabric of society, gave us a certain degree of comfort. We could have peace of mind, knowing that higher values, sacred or religious in turn, had a stable ground to rise up from.

Yet at the same time, I am reminded that in certain spiritual paths, the lotus is said to arise in the muddy waters of samsara. So in these present conditions, with modern and traditional societies fractured and deeply wounded, I wonder what these muddy waters may produce? The awakening to our condition is now on many more people's minds. I find myself asking: Do we have, paradoxically, even better conditions for awakening in these particularly muddy waters?

Everywhere I go, I hear of people exasperated by the conditions of society. Consider the automated calls that people have to suffer through for hours to get a human voice; the hospitals that treat you like you are one of many on a conveyor belt; and the produce aisles in many stores that boast of large, genetically modified but flavorless fruits and vegetables—for only the well-off seem to have access to tastier produce. Of course, the affluent pay a price to enjoy such things, but now the greatest luxury seems to be the ability to enjoy the 'simple pleasures' of life: time with loved ones, a walk in the woods, a relaxed body and mind, and the chance to set one's eyes on a horizon broader than the screens of our phones and computers.

Despite all the 'advances' we have witnessed in the West, we know there is so much suffering and alienation in society. Individuals often express a deep sense of loneliness and even dissatisfaction with their lives. It is true that modern medicine has prolonged lifespans and prevented illness. Technology has made so many things easier. But happiness or contentment for most seem to be further from reach than ever before.

At the same time, religious structures, both in the West and East, are often either becoming more superficial, or are getting radicalized. Fundamentalism is on the rise in all religions, as people with negative motivations take advantage of the new gaping voids in society and governing systems to spread a message that may veer into hatred and discrimination.

Perhaps, if we were to develop a genuine quality of care, things could be different. So it is important to see how we might consciously develop the quality of care, and consider its deeper implications for society.

Caring seems to have many different dimensions. On one level, to care is to love and understand the needs of others, in what we could call a 'horizontal' way. Fundamentally, to care requires us to first be aware: to be aware of our surroundings, to be in-tune with the needs of others. The awareness of the cry of suffering, the alertness of the immediacy of disruption, disjuncture, imbalance, or pain is one fundamental aspect of the quality of care.

In these cases of horizontal care, I care for my fellow being, neighbor, other sentient beings, even perhaps the gardens, or spaces I inhabit. I care for the situation at hand and seek to understand what might give greater comfort and ease, greater beauty and clarity to those around me.

The second, perhaps less known form of care is a 'vertical' kind of care. This form of care may be care for a higher purpose, or even a transcendent, perhaps non-visible one. In this vertical form of care, I imagine that we care for things along an arc of the past and future that may be beyond our present moment. We care about our ancestors and the environment from which we are born. We care about the lakes and the mountains and the sky, for we know that they are our progenitors. We also care about qualities and ideals of our future embodiment. We care about realizing our potential, and the potential of each and every sentient being.

With this form of care, prayer and especially virtuous aspirations, we may find care to be a very powerful vehicle of self-transformation.

We know that within each being a light is there to manifest, and we seek every way to help cultivate their awakening. With our hands folded at the heart level, we pray consciously for their awakening. The horizontal care we extend to our brothers and sisters in the present moment naturally awakens the call for the vertical form of care.

To care means to make one's own life an example of good conduct. It does not mean that we must give big speeches or write fancy words; our actions should simply demonstrate our ideals. Perhaps even more importantly, our care should be evident even when no one is there to see us or congratulate us. Our lives should be our records.

To embody the quality of care is to have a heightened sense of awareness and empathy that moves further and further out from our own immediate surroundings. Our sense of care evolves as we become less and less attached to the sense of the object that we are helping or caring for. The sense of care as a flow, as a natural response to the cries of the world, big or small, is the food to nourish our heart. We can see the good signs of a caring attitude when it begins to feel effortless.

It is natural for caregivers to feel at times over-burdened and burnt-out, as if there is an endless need that cannot be satisfied with one's own resources. In my experience, it is important at these moments to take a pause and learn to re-generate the open-heart feeling that is requisite for healthy caring. In order for caring to have the light quality of *effortless love*, the caregiver must also feel at ease, spacious and in the flow. She should take pauses as needed and learn to replenish her energy and do work in intervals. As she learns to be aware of her expanding ability to care, then those intervals will naturally become shorter and shorter in duration.

In order to offer care to others, it's important to have an understanding of one's own state of mind. When you understand your own mind, you become more accurate, less clumsy, in the kind and quality of care you offer to others. We may not understand why there are times when the people we seek to help actually become up-set, or fail to appreciate our attempts to care for them. In these cases, it has been my experience to let the situation rest a little, to offer a pause and try to better understand what kind of care is needed. Sometimes, the simple offer of space and time, especially for family members and close friends, can help to realign the connection to a place of care.

To care is to understand deeply about what is needed for the other. From this quality of caring, comes forth a deeper embodiment of a life grounded in wholeness and well-being for all. Extending a quality of caring across all boundaries of time and space allows for sentient beings to embody the ideals of all the great Bodhisattvas, saints, and yogis. To be free from the eight worldly dharmas; to live simply, yet heroically, neither discouraged by the magnitude of the world's suffering, nor disheartened by the seeming aloneness of the work, is to rest joyfully in an open heart, ready to serve the needs of others spontaneously, naturally, effortlessly, and perfectly. The activity of caring is a crowning jewel of what it means to be human.

Careful Negotiations

Even if we do not succeed at first, we must not give up on ourselves and our mission of caring. If we give up, we are saying there is nothing left. If caring is left behind, humanity and hope are exhausted.

Therefore, even if you encounter obstacles that prevent your efforts from coming to fruition, try to make a difference in any way you can. Improve your communication; gentle your thoughts; appreciate your sense-impressions and your perceptions. At least you yourself can be all right; at least you can guarantee that you don't have trouble personally.

Maybe you can't help everyone. But secretly, internally, you can determine to open negotiations between your own heart and head.

When the heart says "Yes, great," the head does not necessarily agree. What's happening may be superficial, after all. As we conduct these negotiations—as we engage our own internal regimes—we can continue to look for common ground. Perhaps we are trying to be stewards of the natural world and protect our environment. This is a tall order, and we may not always see the success we long for. But we can always take care of our own, inner environment. For example, we can take better care of the micro-biome of our gut bacteria. If we experience real harmony, keeping ourselves free of stress twenty-four hours a day, these tiny creatures that care for us so steadfastly will respond in kind.

We don't want to bombard ourselves with our failures, assaulting our own bodies and minds with stress and anger. If none of our plans work out, if none of our projects come to fruition, at least we can harmonize our own head and heart, and celebrate our embodiment here and now.

I promise, I will always search for ways to make peace between my own warring factions. At the very least, we can negotiate a break in the conflict—a ceasefire. Perhaps we can do even better than that.

I promise… I won't let these peace talks break down.

Caring Response

When our hearts are full of caring, it is time to respond: with good gestures, good advice, and good direction. It is time to teach others to care, always respecting the circumstances they are in. Teach them with your sincerity, your cooperation, your advice, and your awareness.

You can respond directly, in the first person, saying "This is my experience," and sharing with them: "This is what I did." Remember that you may learn much from the people you are imagining that you teach. Certainly, new understanding will arise, new treasures of knowledge that can make good contributions to your own development.

Deep satisfaction comes from sharing in this way. If we can be helpful, if we can make a difference, if there is a move away from the tragic, away from pain and waste—we are richly rewarded. Our investment has paid off. Our education—our painstaking study of caring—has been worth it.

We do not require fame, money or position. We know that great successes, tremendously helpful discoveries, are possible without any of these things. Ever-expanding caring is the real reward.

When we enjoy the fruits of our caring, it becomes easy to be grateful. It becomes easy to say:

> *Thank you, caring, for giving birth to this wisdom, these blessings. Thank you for supporting us. Thank you, caring, for not giving up. Thank you for sustaining me: your methods are working. Thank you for your sincere efforts: they have brought results.*
>
> *Thank you for caring.*

Caring's Anthem

> Caring knows every place—
> but caring knows no position.
>
> Caring is not afraid to get its hands dirty,
> working in the sun.
>
> Caring loves methods, and the joy of
> broader knowledge.
>
> Caring does not rule or discriminate.

If there is caring, nobody will have to go lower;
nobody will ever get bullied or beaten up.

Caring is wisdom; wise caring
prevents problems.

Caring can take care of impatience.

Caring can prevent not-knowing;
This sublime knowing could be knowable
because I try and do not give up.

This is the heart of my caring: what I know,
I practice.

I am not ready to give up.

My caring is continuity, wisdom
and compassion.

Caring continues, on behalf of body and mind.

Time is precious: I need to take care,
constantly.

Caring with consistency is not a concept.
Embody it! I will, too.

To promote caring, we need to listen.
We need to listen to what the problem is.

We need to look at why there is trouble:
Trees are falling down. Garbage is not picked
up. People are yelling and screaming, people
are in pain.

This is the heart of my caring:
what I know, I practice.

I am not ready to give up.

Look: look around. Listen to them,
for they are your friends.

Investigate the motivations.

Ask: What are they looking for,
what do they want to say?

What is the position they take?
What are the claims staked,

and what the consequences?

What is ignorance doing here;
what is missing?

And we, when we look at them:
what are *we* missing?

What misinterpretation, what tortured
self wastes away in chains?

When we feel sympathy, sorrow,
we are beginning to invite caring.

We can be like hunters, searching:
what is the problem?

Someone does not know why they are unhappy.

You track it down: it's because of lack of care,
because of ignorance.

They lost their hearts, their heads, and
they don't even know.

There's work to do, but we'll get them back.

This is the heart of my caring:
what I know, I practice.

I am not ready to give up.

The Wisdom of Caring

Caring goes to the root of suffering, and it can carry us to the pinnacle of understanding.

Caring is Special Medicine

We often think of caring as something to help alleviate suffering: we care when we make repairs, or when we look after the sick.

Or else we think of caring as something to improve life: we show our care by growing or cooking food, paying attention to the needs of others. This kind of caring can become the motivating force for social harmony.

But caring can do more than soothe or improve: it can remove suffering. It has the power to do this because it is the antidote, not to suffering, but to *ignorance*, the root of suffering.

A Long History

How much suffering have human beings endured in their long history? We can imagine the hunger, fear, yearning, and frustration our species must have known from our earliest emergence into a world we could sense and be affected by, but rarely control.

Some ten thousand years ago, our ancestors built the first towns and cultivated the first fields. Religious ideas began to be codified. Five thousand years ago, the first complex cultures arose, and soon human beings lived within structured economies governed by hierarchies and held in place by laws.

Along with this cultural complexity came inter-cultural conflict. Empires arose, established through trade relationships and military might. They struggled, grew, changed, and collapsed. Some have disappeared so entirely that scarcely a trace of their ancient power remains.

The large-scale conflicts that mark human history have been matched every step of the way by interpersonal conflicts at the social and familial level.

And through all this turmoil, traced in the records kept by our forebears, deep within us were the same wars, fought on silent battlefields of heart and mind.

Those battles are raging still.

Education and Progress

Many of us have learned to regard our human history as a story of gradual improvements; it is a popular idea in the West. The ideal of progress rests on the assumption that the ancient world lacked fundamental knowledge we have since acquired. In our progress-version of history, we have cured terrifying diseases, banished pests and predators from our homes, vastly reduced the need for physical labor, and devised ways of life and forms of government that extend benefits to an ever-expanding population, in ever-widening circles of care. We have turned deserts into green oases, and made wildernesses into pasture-lands, feeding billions of people.

These are unquestionably positive developments.

But these same developments have brought unexpected side-effects. Our very attempts to control the natural world seem to result in nature getting out of control. Today, we witness profound imbalances that affect the world's natural systems at a deep level. Changes in the oceans; the loss of the polar ice caps; droughts, storms, extreme weather events that occur more and more frequently: these are becoming commonplace. Many of our largest and most prosperous cities are oppressive and even dangerous to live in, and all over the world human beings struggle with pollution, over-crowding, violence, widespread illness and chronic poverty. Along with these troubles has come the normalization of deeply selfish ways of life, and the enshrinement at the heart of society of attitudes that harm us all.

The severe consequences of our impulse to control and improve nature suggest that our 'progress' ideal warrants a closer look.

Mind's Power Overlooked

Space has no defined location of its own—but space provides a place for shape and form to manifest. We know space is necessary, but we can't point to it.

In a sense, mind is like this too. We see its manifestations—feel the effects of its decisions—but we cannot point to mind itself, try as we might.

Even as our knowledge has developed, growing more and more involved and precise over time, it continues to be based on a set of fundamental oppositions between subject and object, self and other, individual and environment. This is the mind's way of understanding things.

We might be very surprised to realize how much of the world we know—its contents, qualities, flavors, distinctions, 'truths,' and 'realities'—is the result of mind's discriminating, pattern-identifying, and orienting activities. Mind may be woven far more deeply into the fabric of reality than we realize.

At one time, religion had a place in daily life; spiritual paths offered us a way to make space for and give respect to an invisible power. In modern times, we have largely lost the vocabulary that would allow us to talk about such things. Perhaps this is one reason we have trouble understanding or even recognizing the existence of mind and its activities: the very idea that something invisible can produce effects has become rather alien.

What we today call the progress of knowledge is the elaboration and proliferation of visible, palpable, *knowable* characters, all of which appear thanks to a frame of concepts provided by mind; but mind itself never comes into view. Both our education and the fruits of this education are part of this frame.

Knowledge that remains on this level, within this frame, cannot discover its own point of arising. Unaware of its own origins, it may not be able to envision a way to become free from its limitations.

If we feel skeptical of the role played by mind, we might hypothesize that the world is definitively distinct from mind—that mind has played no part in its production whatsoever. But without our minds, there is no way to identify any elements that would supposedly exist independently of mind and its identifications. Indeed, we cannot even conduct the experiment.

In any pointing, any showing of things or their absence, mind is involved. In any situation that has noticeable features—features that can be distinguished, labeled, named—mind plays a part.

Mind discerns order or the absence of order in the universe. We could even say that 'order' is mind's own creation, a name it gives to patterns it perceives. Mind focuses on happy, healthy things—or the opposite. It divides the world into 'good' and 'bad,' plus and minus, positive and negative. The judge of all this, without a doubt, is mind.

Mind sorts the pros and cons, the rich and poor, evaluating them all. The flavors and qualities that give our life's journey its character are all manifestations of mind, expressions of its decisions.

Perhaps it is helpful to think of our journey as a kind of tour. It reminds us that our experience is, in a sense, packaged for us.

What we see is conditioned by the fact that *it is seen.* It is something to look at—a presentation whose character as a presentation cannot be disentangled from what it presents. Our experience boils down to what we take in: what we notice. On this journey, we travelers too are in transit, and mind is responsible for the tour and the tourist alike.

Mind, in that sense, *makes everything matter.*

A sense of mind runs like a thread through all our experience: we detect its trace in our perceptions, where it is hard to disentangle judgments from observations. Mind is *in* experience, holding it all together, creating the connections that permit the associations that build the relationships that form the structures that we, by long force of habit, give the name 'shape and form.'

Throughout history, throughout our own personal pasts, it has happened this way; it will happen again; it is *happening right now.*

So let's ask: Where is this happening? Who is talking? Is it the thinker we identify as 'my mind?' Is it some kind of observer?

Would *you* answer yes, or no?

If yes, then where is it, and how do we know it is there? If no, how do we know that? Who observed the absence of the observer?

> *Who cares?*
>
> *Oh, come now, don't try to play it cool. I care, and you do too.*
>
> *But we can still ask this:*
>
> *Who cares? And for the sake of whom?*

Mind the Mover

Mind is the one in control. It pronounces the way things are, and issues its proclamations. In the play of mind, my role is to be the receiver, the one who hears and responds. You could say that as I respond, I make use of the mind, but this does not mean that now I am in charge. It is mind that controls and makes use of mind. Gradually continuity is established, and an order takes form: the regime of mind.

The kind of care that can free us from mind's regime has nothing to do with trying to collect a few more crumbs of positivity, a few more moments when we can say that we feel truly satisfied. The care we need is more like a healing ointment that soothes and gently releases the tension that has tightened our aching muscles and ligaments into knots.

It starts with acknowledging the core patterns that have shaped our experience: the division into subject and object, the unthinking reliance on 'from' and 'to', the reality of our anger and disappointment. It is here that care is needed. We need a way to work with mind.

Mind knows how to bring us problems, but is that all it can do? It offers logic and clever ways of classifying; it shows us the consequences of our actions; it urges us to be rational. All that is helpful, but it will not solve the problems that mind stirs up. In fact, mind uses rea-

son as a kind of weapon—almost a form of torture. It
proceeds by stealth, speaking in soft, measured tones:

> *You have had no success in your efforts; you have
> failed at your responsibilities.*

> *No one respects you or really cares for you, and
> you have failed completely at caring for yourself.*

> *I will show you why. I will lay out all the expla-
> nations, and in the end you will have to admit
> that you have only yourself to blame. Don't you
> see? Your situation is hopeless.*

> *Anyway, what right do you have to think you can
> make fundamental changes? The problems you
> are facing now are the same ones faced by human
> beings through history. Do you think the early
> cave dwellers had it any better? Can you find
> evidence that early civilizations had different
> ways to live? Do indigenous peoples, living
> simpler but more brutal ways of life, show you
> a different model?*

> *There are really no solutions. The situation is
> hopeless. Far better to follow the rules I have
> laid down. In fact, you have no choice.*
> *You have to do it.*

There is no point in arguing with the mind when it
speaks to us this way. And yet, we should not turn our
backs on mind. Indeed, we cannot. Mind has its own
logic, and it makes sense for us to go along with it, to

make use of mind's way of proceeding and the information it offers us.

Although we do not have to accept its conclusions, we can cooperate with mind. Where there seems to be no ground for cooperation, we can negotiate.

When mind points out our difficulties and traces out their causes, we should pay close attention. It is true that all sentient beings experience suffering and confusion. It is true that we are the victims of our circumstances and conditioning. It is true that we live in a world shaped by causality, and that our situation, seen in that light, seems hopeless. These are important points to acknowledge and reflect on, to take to heart, so that care grows within us.

Still, there is a more basic question to ask, and care will help us see its significance.

> *I see the truth of the patterns mind points out,*
> *and I accept that. I swallow whole the explana-*
> *tions mind so patiently offers, as though that*
> *were my only choice. I take on the identity mind*
> *offers me, never thinking things might be differ-*
> *ent. I do what mind tells me to do, even though I*
> *can see that following that path leads nowhere.*
> *I accept what mind tells me, as though I had*
> *been drugged into compliance, and I take on*
> *and embody its truths.*
>
> *Why is this so?*

169

Mind is the initiator, the promoter, the conductor, but it has nothing to offer me but more problems, more difficulties. Why do I go along? This way of living is not acceptable.

Then what holds me back from changing it? The answer is simple: I have not learned to care.

Caring and the Shadow of Mind

Mind's expressions and manifestations are like shadows cast; their existence points to a kind of caster. But at the same time, that which appears as shape and form is only apparent because it blocks the light.

These shapes and forms, then, could be connected to a kind of ignorance, a limit set by mind on perceiving and knowing. When mind decides, something is *cast,* and released from the language-mold to really inhabit the world. At the same time, something is *cast away,* relegated to the background.

Caring communicates with what mind's judgments cannot embrace. It is an antidote to the ignorance that signs off on *this* shape, *this* form, *this reality.*

Caring Comes First

Caring comes before the truths that mind proclaims, and caring is where our challenge to the regime of mind must originate.

Before the first message arrives, at the edge of the edge, we can care. A signal is sent, but before that signal, a wave is generated. That is what we need to neutralize. We can stop the bullet before it strikes—catch the arrow before it hits the target.

> *I know all the reasons for the status quo; I know where all this is headed. But because I care, I do not have to go along dumbly. I do not have to play the role of receiver.*

When I care, I see that it is possible to negotiate. For the mind's regime to operate, for the pain I have accepted for so long to be activated, many circumstances must come together. For this, my cooperation is needed. I have been trained to give it unthinkingly, never even imagining that I could do otherwise. But when I care, I understand that the choice is mine.

While we live in the regime, we are the losers. It is like a business that is subject to so many taxes that there is no possibility of making a profit. Running this way, we are always in the red. We lose our time and our energy. We lose the knowledge available to us. We lose the possibility for real joy. We lose the opportunity to bond with others who share the universal burdens of pain and suffering, of getting lost in thoughts, concepts, and emotionality.

Now, however, we know. We can pronounce the truth. Knowing for ourselves how to care, we can resist the power of the regime. We can express clearly what is happening, and we can trace how the structures that bind us have been set up. Space is available, time is available, and knowledge is available. If we can only care, everything we encounter is open; nothing has been shut down.

A Caring Conversation

Modern cultures place a high value on education as the key to success, and that certainly makes sense. However, education is not the whole story. If we truly want to be successful in this journey through life, the benefit we can get through reading books or through years of study at top quality schools will not be enough.

Instead, we must develop with the greatest care the inner knowledge that lets us make the most of any situation. Concepts and ideas are fine, but they do not really go to the heart of what we need. What is the use of eating enormous amounts of food if what we put in our mouths and bellies does not really nourish the body?

My own conclusion, based on my own experience, may be overly simple, but I present it here because I believe it has something of importance to offer. I would put it like this: whatever knowledge we rely on, *mind is the one responsible for what we know.*

Mind is the agent for knowledge, the collector of knowledge. It is the one who guides us on our journey.

It promotes our activities and it sets the course we follow. It is mind that determines whether we will succeed or fail, whether we will experience happiness or unhappiness. We may have great accomplishments and perfect training, but what we do with our lives seems to depend on mind.

Knowing this, we could imagine having a dialogue with mind. Things have not always gone well for us, and it is time to negotiate a better relationship between the self and mind.

Self: I have always followed your lead. I have given my best, and I have been completely obedient. You give me instructions, and I do what you say. But now I think we have to do it differently. It's time for us to talk things over. Now it's up to you to show a little cooperation.

Mind: What did you have in mind?

Self: Let's start with the basics. I think you have to agree that all your orders, all your directions, have not always worked out to my benefit. Sure, I've had some good times, and I give you credit for that. But you have also given me hard times. I know a lot about loneliness and anxiety. I know what it's like to act in neurotic ways. I know about all kinds of mental suffering: guilt and pain and just plain negativity.

Mind: So what? You're just describing what everybody experiences. That's just how life is. What makes you think I have anything to do with it?

Self: Before I might have gone along with that, but no more. The way I see it, you're like a software engineer. You upload a new program, and I dutifully start running the program. I may choose what moves to make, but it all happens inside the program. In the end, you're the one responsible.

Mind: That's a nice enough story, but I hope you realize it's just a story. You're focused on the negative, but I don't think you realize how much I've done for you.

Self: I'm not saying you haven't done some good things too. I'm willing to grant you that you had a hand in whatever I know. It's thanks to you that I have the data or information that I rely on. But you're missing the point. My experience is made up of some things that are positive and some that are negative. If you really cooperated—if you really cared for me at a deep level—you would turn my experience toward what's good for me.

Mind: And how do I do that? Just what is it you expect from me?

Self: If you cared, you would help me shape a journey toward healing and well-being. You would give more insight into the operation of my senses. You would help me care.

Mind: It seems to me that you're blaming me for problems you're bringing on yourself. How can you hold me responsible when you're the one who keeps making bad decisions?

Self: Am I really making the decisions, or are you? It seems to me that I'm just following the script that you give me. I have to give you credit: you had a pretty nice strategy going. You kept telling me that I was the one in charge, that I was the one at the center of everything. And I'll admit it; I fell for it. I liked the feeling of self-importance. But all the time, you were the one pulling the strings.

Mind (chuckles): Yes, you do get quite a kick out of being Mr. Important.

Self: Guilty as charged. But who made sure that I reacted the way I did? Who set me up to insist on my identity? For a long time, I didn't even see there was a question there to be asked. But now I know that you were in charge all the time.

Maybe it's because I care more deeply now. I can see where this is headed.

Mind: I don't notice you giving me credit for suddenly having the scales fall from your eyes. Your analysis seems a little one-sided.

Self: I'll take credit for my own caring, thank you! The point is, I really worked for it. This is not just me following some script—the 'Now I see' script. If you were still the one calling all the shots, I'd still be operating in the dark—I guarantee it.

Mind: Now that you can see so clearly—at least that's what you claim—why don't you tell me just *how* I've been going about tricking you all this time? What makes me so smart? Or maybe I should ask, what makes you so dumb? It takes two to get fooled, you know.

Self: I agree completely: it takes two to get fooled. I'm not going to play that game anymore. That's why it's time for you and me to come to a different working arrangement.

Mind: And what exactly is your idea of what would have to change?

Self: The way I see it, your basic maneuver is to manifest the triple-threat team of 'I', 'me', and 'mine'. You dictate instructions, but to whom do they go? They go to 'me'. You issue orders, and who carries them out? It's 'I'. You set out the way things are, and who accepts ownership and confirms what you've laid out? It's 'mine'. You lay down the rules, and then it's up to me to operate within them. It's a wonder I can ever have an original thought. But somehow it is possible. I have been able to find the gaps in the story you are telling.

Mind: How do you know you've succeeded? Maybe you've just found some new variation on a theme that I've made available. Not that I'm accepting your claims! I'm just saying that you keep falling into the same contradiction. You say that I set everything up, but now you've been able to find a way out. How does that happen?

Self: You set the course I take. It's like asking someone for directions and then setting out along the road they point to. I can go here and there; I can go faster or slower; I can take a break when I want to, but I keep going along the same road.

Mind: And now you've found a new road? That seems unlikely.

Self: No, that's just the point. It's not that I need to follow a new road. I've realized now that I can just put down the map and look around me with new eyes.

Mind: What kind of roads do you see yourself following?

Self: The ones we've been talking about. 'I' is a road; 'me' is a road; 'mine' is a road. Identity is a road, and so is soul.

Mind: So you're ready to set all that aside, to drop it like a backpack that's gotten too heavy to carry. I wonder what you'll find when you do. Without a map, do you really expect to get anywhere?

Self: I'm not saying I don't need your help. I can't really imagine what it would be like not to be able to rely on mind. I'm just saying that it's time for us to become partners, working together.

Mind: This whole picture you've been presenting makes no sense to me. We're already a team. You get an idea in your head—like this silly idea that we need to change our relationship—but where does that idea come from if not from me?

So, I say: Fine, let's partner up. That's no problem, because the way I see it we've been partners all along.

Self: Being partners would mean that we're equals. But that's a joke! The way we've done things till now, you make all the rules.

Mind: Let's say you're right, and that we need to make a new agreement and set up a new working relationship. What would that mean in concrete terms?

Self: I want you to agree to act on my behalf. I want you to care for me, to give me good advice when I need it; to point me in the right direction when that is what I need.

Let's be clear. I'm not saying you don't care for me at all. I don't believe I have could have become what I am without your caring. But there have also been times when you don't care for me at all. I know that things never go exactly the way anybody expects or hopes. But I have learned from you to accept a lot of things that I realize now didn't have to be that way. That's all over and done with now. I just need your cooperation.

Mind: What makes you so sure that I'm the one in control—that I have all the power? I have seen you take credit for what you do countless times, but I don't often hear you saying, "Oh, it wasn't me that did that. Mind did it."

Self: I do share some of the responsibility. Now that I realize that caring is the best way to be, I understand that I need to develop my own care. But if you care, you can show me how to care. Let's do it together!

The reason I keep saying that you're in control is that without me, experience would still go on. The eyes can see; the ears can hear. It doesn't take self to make that happen. But it does take mind. At least . . . I think so.

'Self' seems to me a story I tell, but I'm not sure whether 'self' is really the best story available. I have gotten used to the idea that I'm the same self now that I was a dozen years ago, or when I was a tiny baby, but does that really make sense? All I have to go on are some memories.

Mind: I'd say you've stopped making sense. If you're just a story, what business do you have wanting to negotiate with me? It's like trying to do business with a ghost. "Sign right here, Mr. Ghost."

Self: You might have a point, except that I'm not so sure about you either. That's what made me hesitate a moment ago. I've gotten used to thinking of mind as the one that organizes everything and sets it all in motion, but what if that's a story too? If you're going to dismiss me as nothing but a story, I'm ready to say the same about you.

Mind: So I'm a story and you're a story. Well, let's suppose that's true. Still, one of us is telling another story—a story about who's responsible for your situation. Why tell that story? Did you decide to get out of bed this morning? Do you choose what you want to read or what you want for breakfast? Did you choose to have this conversation? Why blame me for all that?

Self: That's the story, all right. I do this and I don't do that; I like this and don't like that. That's my way of making sense of the world. But it's not as though that story just popped up in this moment. When I tell that story, I'm playing out the I-script. I make sense of the world because I am following out your rules of interpretation. Your story and your rules. That's how I make sense of the world, because that's how you have proclaimed things to be. You know, this present moment doesn't just appear by magic. It grows out of the past. And it seems that you have shaped that past to suit your purposes, not mine.

Mind: I'd say you're still turning your own shortcomings and weakness into a story about my having all the power. So tell me: where does that story come from?

Self: I'm not just basing this on my own experience. I can see what's going on in the world, and I can study history. The evidence is right there. There is nobody on earth who hasn't suffered. There is nobody who hasn't had their share of trouble—not just because of circumstances and conditions, but because of the patterns you have set up.

Blame me for my own problems if you want, but it's not just me. Everyone suffers from the same situation.

Mind: That's because everyone is in it for themselves. Everyone is trying to advance their own selfish interests. Everyone puts the self at the center. That's not my doing.

Self: Ah, but it is. We don't know any other way. You've set it up like that: you and your regime. We just go along. You can't say that's our choice, because we have never learned that we could do it differently. And that's your doing. When it comes right down to it, you don't really care about me or about anyone.

Mind: Tell me: just what do you think I get out of all this? If you suffer, I suffer along with you. If you feel limited or trapped, don't you think I experience the same feelings? Why would I want to promote your suffering? What good does that do me?

Self: I know that when I play by the rules you dictate, when I live in the regime that you have set up, I will suffer. I'm the one who has emotional ups and downs. I'm the one who gets caught up in neurotic, obsessive worries and concerns, judging myself and judging others, never satisfied. But I'm not so sure you share in those kinds of experiences! If the king imposes a steep tax on his peasants, they're the ones who have to do all the back-breaking work to bring in the harvest and pay the tax collector. Does the king suffer the same way they do? Does he wake up in the morning with his back aching and his limbs on fire? I don't think so.

Mind: But you haven't answered the question. What's the benefit to me when you suffer?

Self: You may not care whether I suffer or not. That's what I've been saying—you haven't shown that you really care about me. So on that level, you may be neutral, which I would say is not a good thing. But to answer your question, here's what you get out of it: you stay in charge. You're the one running things, laying things out, proposing and disposing. I can feel the pull of that: it's nice to be in charge. But my guess is that for you, it's not just nice; it's a kind of absolute necessity. If you're not the ruler, it's as though you don't even exist.

I'm not saying you want to see me suffer; it's more that you don't care whether I suffer. But you do care that I stick around and that I play by your rules. That's want I want to see changed. I long for you to care about me, not just about you. And I have the feeling that if you cared, then between us, we could do remarkable things.

Mind: So just what it is that you want me to do?

Self: I want you to fully engage. I want you to participate in my experience. It may mean opening new channels of communication. It may be that you need to connect more with the heart. Maybe that's how we can find a better way of cooperating.

Until now, I had the sense that something was wrong, that somebody was playing a trick on someone, but I could never see it clearly. But now I've studied how you operate, and I've observed my own reactions and the reactions of everyone around me, and I see that I was naïve. I have been fooled, but I won't be fooled again.

The past is gone; history is history. But the future lies open. So I demand that you act differently. I insist on your care, for me and for all of us who have lived so long in your regime. I am not willing to go along with the restrictions you have put in place. I am not willing to settle for the limited forms of knowledge you allow. I am the knower, and the knower needs to know. Can't you care for us? Can't you allow for new knowledge? Can't you support us, so we can break through our limitations?

Mind: Suppose it's true; suppose that you've been living within a restricted zone, accepting limitations that I've set in place. Don't tell me that you don't get something out of it. I put you in the center; I put you in charge. You decide and you name. You set the tone. That's worth a lot, don't you think? If I set things up, I'd say that you have been my accomplice. If I'm the king, you're the minister.

Self: Don't try to be so clever. It's 'I' that's your minister—I and me and mine. True, I went along, but that's because you wrote the script. But now that's over and done with. I won't play along anymore.

Mind: And what would you want to see put in its place?

Self: I want to see new channels of communication opening, channels that transmit peace and calm and harmony. I want liberation beyond control. For that, I need your help—I need your care. You have set up a regime where I am like a slave, not in charge of my own destiny. It doesn't matter whether I act in the name of truth or the name of reality or in the name of mind and what it knows. However, you frame it, I end up in a no-choice realm.

That's what needs to change. You know what I mean: the pain, the worries, the loneliness. I've had enough. But I need your help.

Mind: I ask again, what do you expect from me?

Self: You could start by admitting your responsibility. Here we all are, in this beautiful world that is constantly displaying its riches, a bounty of blessings. Yet on the inside, everything is shut down, closed, tight. The beauty and joy that I feel from time to time disappear almost immediately, and I find myself going here and there, eyes tight, body tense.

Mind: And you say that's my fault.

Self: Yes, I hold you responsible. But I am sure you can help change it all. All I want from you is to care. I'm sure that I can get out from under this dictatorship. Will you help me?

Mind: It still seems more like your problem than mine. You keep talking about your feelings. What I am supposed to do about how you feel?

Self: Because I am sure that what I feel has to do with opening to a greater sense of knowing, and that is your special domain. With your cooperation, I could open the magnetic power of showing and revealing, of sharing and exhibiting. Those are the operators.

Could we meet in that place of knowing? Could we explore the mechanisms together? I have so many questions, and I know you can help me look into them. How is appearance allocated? How can we share? What is doing the pointing? If you have been tricking me, are you willing to reveal your tricks? I will share if you will; I will show if you will. Don't you want to go beyond this endless play, this constant misdirection?

Mind: Yes, I do see some possibilities.

Self: Good! I know you know what I'm talking about. I have been watching closely, and now I see, so you can see too. I have been ignorant and innocent. I have not known how to care; I have lived in darkness, missing out on the shining light of care. But now you can help. We can go forward together.

For now I know this: you need caring too. You have your own role—the role of dictator. But that is not enough. There is more for you to know. If you care for me, I can care for you.

The One Who Cares

Above mind, beyond mind; above the senses, beyond the senses; before reality is cast into solid forms: there is that which cares.

What is it? We have never been introduced. It seems it is a self-kept secret. Mind itself does not seem to know.

Perhaps it is a higher part of mind, but if so, the lower part of mind, the one that regulates the regime, seems to have no access—and no such capability.

How might we describe this kindness-mind, even conditionally? Let us say: an aura of light, an open place, like the sun rising at dawn... or the light before dawn breaks. Neutral, free of all belonging. Independent and uniquely powerful. Subject to no dictation, free from all suggestion. A higher authority.

Mind's regime is like the lower courts in the system of justice, dutifully applying the laws, but strangely never truly knowing where their authority to enter judgments comes from. This is the territory of the presupposed, where self-liberation is an impossible dream.

Caring answers to a higher authority. In caring, there is no belonging to the established order.

"Above mind." 'Above' means beyond the mind of regime: beyond subjectivity and the contents of experience, beyond identification and the claims of the ego, beyond emotionality. It means a different realm, not attached to the sensory reality that the mind proclaims.

We should not be confused by the ordinary meaning of the words we use. 'Above' is like flying, but not in the way that an airplane or spaceship flies. 'Beyond' means beyond the immediate instant, but not in a way that leaves something behind. 'Higher authority' does not suggest a dictatorship that must be overthrown or claims of ownership that must be resisted.

'Above and beyond' does not happen just once, like a rocket that breaks free of earth's gravity to enter the vastness of space. It is 'happening' all the time, both before and after. It is circles of time, beginnings of time, endings of time. That is what it means to care.

Until we know care from within, all this is mysterious, but it need not stay that way. Once we have the experience of care, preserving contact is not difficult, and it becomes natural to embody care. At that time, love, compassion, mutual respect, and meaningfulness all find expression. We no longer need to hope and dream, to imagine some distant, faraway place and time. When we confirm care, we find ourselves in a better place, a higher place, a place where we are free.

That place is not elsewhere. Through care, subject and object are transformed, and the ordinary, stuck world, just as it is, becomes the open realm of care.

To be in care is to abandon all skepticism and uncertainty. Once you recognize the realm of care, once you are within it, you gain total, unstoppable confidence. There is no longer any need for effort. There is no job that needs to be done, and no further need for distinctions into right and wrong, near and far.

Do you wish you could be more aware? It is no longer necessary. Do you wish you could cultivate compassion? There is no need. Do you wonder how you will ever get from here to there, ever leave your old patterns behind and enter into a new way of being? None of that holds up, not in the usual ways. All the prepositions—the 'from' and 'to' and 'in' and 'out' and 'before' and 'after' and 'of'—are set aside. The truths of directionality no longer apply, and there is no polarity.

Living our ordinary lives, we go here and there. Our routines and concerns are pedestrian. We make do with a limited budget and worry about filling our stomachs with food we really like. We exercise and worry about our health. We scratch our itches and pursue our desires. We shriek and laugh and cry. We fantasize and imagine and regret, and we plan for the future. From within care, it all looks very temporary, like a tent erected on a windy bluff. Caring, we find ourselves in an open place. *In* caring, acting from a caring vision, there is no place to travel, and nowhere we must go.

How can we get to this place where 'getting there' no longer matters? It is a strange sort of question to ask, for as soon as I ask, all possibility of real answers vanishes. Language, concepts, and perceptions take over, making it certain that there is no way to arrive at care. How could there be? I make my usual judgments and download my usual experience. I do my best to figure out this and that. I make the results the basis of what I do next, but all the while I only confirm that I am once again working within the structures of the regime.

With great diligence, I try to fix things up, to make improvements. But my efforts will never lead to care if I do not look 'behind' the workings of the regime. Where did this situation come from? How did it develop? How does the instant occur?

It is all a magical show, this reality we take for granted. One instant arises very much like the last. How is that arising possible? We cannot say; we are not aware. Worse, we do not even ask. The magic is still there, but we make use of it in our own restricted and impoverished ways. We confirm what is established and judge it to be good or bad. We assign labels and pronounce the truth of what we have identified. We choose the good over the bad and the right over the wrong and think we are getting somewhere. Yet in the end, our progress proves illusory.

Playing without Care

Our lives consist of so many activities, so many interests and concerns, so many matters to be sorted out as we judge appropriate. We go in search of wealth and power and beauty. We seek the most refined philosophies, the most engaging and moving works of art, the most stirring music. We work through the complexities of our lives like skilled players absorbed in a chess match. Roles and rules have been set up, and various determined orders prevail: logical, mathematical, scientific, philosophical and so on. Yet all these orders seem conditional. The conditions have to do with mind.

The inherent structures of our lives establish what can be so. Working out the implications, we find certain ways to respond and receive. We cultivate certain abilities. We play certain games. There is nothing new here: what we get out is simply the product of what we have put in. Yet we call it knowledge, or even wisdom.

As the games unfold, we claim our small victories. We celebrate positive outcomes, we carve out times for rest and relaxation, we receive and bestow praise. Still, when the game is over, we find ourselves back in the same place we were when we started. And even while we are playing, it seems to be circumstances that are in control more than the skill with which we play. How many of the things we celebrate can truly be said to mark real accomplishment?

If we look closely or see more clearly, countless patterns shape our circumstances. There are the broad patterns of samsara, the patterns of the mind, the patterns that shape language, feelings, and the imagination. The rules that guide our conduct manifest rhythms and transitions, ensuring that each point will connect with every other point, expressing various forms of energy, various relations to time and mind. What benefit can we find from all this?

Living in this way does gives us a richly varied way of life. There are the changes in our own lives, but also the changes that unfold throughout the course of history. One civilization arises, flourishes, and falls, and another takes its place. Different philosophies emerge, and great treatises are written to record forms of understanding that will soon be largely forgotten. Artists, musicians, and statesmen present their own creations, manifesting whatever it is that has stimulated them to produce.

Responding to all this, we cognize and evaluate and try to repeat what we consider to have value. It is like consulting cookbooks that show us how to prepare our favorite cuisine—French, Italian, Chinese, Indian—each with its own taste, character, and substance. Perhaps such possibilities were established by accomplished masters, but now our responses are at a more simple level, registering what we like or do not like.

Like naïve children, we base our choices and reactions on the most superficial dimensions of what presents itself. We receive the communication, we express our liking, and we align ourselves with what is commonly accepted as good or valuable. Like a young teenager playing the latest video game, we are hooked, and our excitement becomes its own reward.

There is something surprising in all this. Someone has set all these structures up—is it mind? Whatever is responsible, it is clever, clever enough to catch us up completely. We give our time and energy to what draws us in, yet how much are we really enjoying the ways we pass time? Have we ever really decided for ourselves that this is the way we want to live?

It may sound as though we are talking here only about the diversions of immature or unsophisticated actors, but this is not the case. Change a few elements, and these descriptions could apply to anyone at any time, carrying out any activity. Captains of industry respond in the same way; teachers—the ones responsible for educating the next generation—are also not immune.

Now, however, we know that what we really need is care, so let us look from that perspective. We have been living our lives without care; we have been care-less. We have decided not to look beneath the surface. We have accepted that seeking profit or fame is what matters, and we settle for playing that game. Whether I am the consumer or the manufacturer, my aim is to win, whether I judge winning in financial terms, social terms, or personal terms. And so I go on. But if I go just the tiniest bit deeper, I may find myself wondering what it all means.

I have lived much of my life this way, perhaps thirty or forty years or longer. Have I really enjoyed the constant pressure, the competition, the worries and concerns? Have I really benefited?

Perhaps this is not the point. Perhaps there is nothing more to my life than playing the role I have been assigned. This is my commitment and my obligation: this is what it means to have an ego and an image. I am loyal to my own personality—how could I not be? I busy myself with working out consistent reasons to justify what I do and the life I live. Intent on that much, I cultivate a certain discipline.

Proceeding on this basis, whatever I do finds its significance in how it fits with my preordained identity. I accomplish my duties and fulfil my responsibilities. In return I find that I feed back to myself a steady diet of desire, selfish concerns, anxiety, and an ongoing struggle for fulfilment and satisfaction. No matter how virtuously I behave, how much benefit will truly result?

Here I am, playing the same roles, caught in the same patterns, manifesting the same energy. My ways of responding are fixed in place: 'should' and 'must' and 'have to be'. My education points me in the same directions. The reality I live is self-confirming, the truth I accept and virtues I pursue are all frozen in place. I cannot find a new way to travel: no ladder I can climb, no rocket I can launch. Anyway, there are no new worlds to discover. Subject interacts with object, and the environment discloses itself in predictable ways. All the complex causalities cooperate.

Is that it? Is that the bottom line?

The Now of Care

What we need now is care. It is good to act in accord with our values, but only if we care will our actions be meaningful.

Care is the place we want to get to: the right place, with no conceptual thoughts, no words or labels. In the open space of care, there is no naming, identification, or position. I do not put forward my point of view, my position, my knowledge, my recognition or achievement, or my possession of the truth of accomplishment. These may not do the job. It is when we care without such props that we embody fully. We do not need these piddling little resources. No ... let it go. Let the wind blow away the clouds.

We live in a world of change. We all know advancing age, and we encounter impermanence on every front. We are not indestructible; in fact, we are vulnerable and transition-able. We base ourselves on circumstances—the biochemistry of our body, the organic realness of the heart, the DNA that patterns our being. And these shapes too are transition-able, moving backward, moving forward. Looking at history, we see how A moves to B and B moves to C, until in the end there is Z, except that it too is no end. Time proceeds in its nanoseconds, and the ripples ripple. We know this, and we believe it too, for we see the changes going on.

So what are we to do? We need a new way. It must be unchangeable, yet it must also be available here and now. There is no comfort in stories of living in the distant future in an everlasting heaven, basking in the sun, on permanent vacation. We have no interest in what will happen 'someday.'

No, this is it, right here and now. No need to prepare for the future; let us prepare instead right in this instant. Distant projects and future hopes may inspire us, but this is not the place and time to wait patiently for the coming of what does not change or decay. 'One day' is no use. We can scratch that off the calendar right now. That is not the caption that this picture needs.

The now of care is not the now of the ticking clock, nor is it the now that we can point to or point out. When we care, now is completely open; it is unified. It has no coming and going, no directions back and forth. Language may speak of a realm of perfection, but it does us no good if it is a 'somewhere else,' a place to go. 'There' and 'here' are not roles for us to play or destinations for us to seek.

In the end, even our sense of journeying is only a temporary idea; we need not concern ourselves with destinations. Treasures are available everywhere, as long as we have the resource of care.

Until now, I have not been treated well, not by myself and not by the circumstances and conditions I have chosen to accept as real. Seeing this truth as it applies to me and my life, I see that we all find ourselves in similar situations. There are patterns we all know well, patterns that no one has been able to penetrate or fix. Scientists, philosophers, performers, humanists: here none of them have anything of value to offer us. They have all missed the point, missed it completely.

It is time to do it differently. It is time, at last, to care.

Caring's Treasure: A Vision

I once had an image come to me: you might say I imagined it. At the beginning, there was a very tiny point, almost infinitesimal. The point expanded. It opened into a pyramid, with the point at the very tip and the edges of the pyramid expanding out and down in four directions. The four legs shaped the pyramid; in our usual way of thinking, we would say that they defined the pyramid's foundation. In my way of seeing, though, it was the point at the top that formed the basis for the pyramid.

It seemed to me that this image of the point and the pyramid stood as a symbol for our human being, with all our faculties and sensory capacities tracing back to that single small point. But I saw it with more specificity than that. In the fantasy that I conceived, the image of the pyramid was linked to a very ancient civilization, active long before the times accessible to our historical records. I imagined that those people, in that long ago time, practiced the truth of a single, all-originating point.

Call it a religion, a philosophy, or simply a transformational way of knowing and being—this deep understanding informed their way of life and made of it something completely dynamic and alive. The pyramid stood for what was permanent and eternal, and their conduct, their view, everything they experienced, and everything they did related back to the pyramid and its originating and sustaining point.

In the Buddhist tradition in which I was raised, we speak of the *vajra*, usually understood as an indestructible diamond or an all-powerful thunderbolt. The vajra, like the point in my fantasy, can be understood as a single, shining point, radiating perfection in all directions, diamond-like in its indestructibility.

The vision of the vajra is beyond our ordinary capacity to see, and the forms that depict the vajra are merely symbolic. Yet the radiant lucency of the diamond gives us a way to imagine what the vajra is meant to express. It is impenetrable, not because of its unsurpassed hardness, but because in the realm of the vajra there is nothing and nobody there. Because it is free from the duality of subject and object, the vajra is sacred.

These images may seem esoteric and inaccessible, but the truth they refer to is a treasure that we already embody, here and now. Our responsibility is to let this treasure be truly known, to bring it into our experience and let it gradually unfold. That is the message I hope to convey when I speak of care.

The development that care enables is not available through direct means. It is not a target we must hit, or a gleaming jewel we must somehow possess. Our approach must be both softer and more skillful.

If we try to name it, relying on language and concepts, we have already missed the mark. If we gesture or point or offer subtle analogies, we will fall into confusion and incomprehension. We are not trying to offer new meanings, even though that is what the regime of mind and its faithful inhabitants demand. We are not presenting a new direction or offering an attractive new investment. If we take these routes, we will only end in misunderstanding and misuse.

From one perspective, we are already too far down the road toward the regime to expect or imagine that we could make any change. It is something like the way our economy is based on the dollar as the measure of value. People work their whole lives to get enough dollars to live on, or to build up a store of dollars that they can pass on to their children or invest in other ways. It is almost crazy, because everyone will tell you that the dollar is just an idea—images on paper, paper promises: a concept that works only because everyone accepts that it works.

Yet work it does, and it has been working for centuries. It works even though we know there was a time when the dollar did not exist, and there are places —even to-day—where people live outside the network of financial interactions. None of that makes any difference. We made it up, but now it rules our lives. We created it, but now we serve it. Within that framework, care may not have a major role to play.

Now, however, we can do it differently. There are other dimensions of being, secret and sacred, having nothing to do with our established orders.

The outside world looks at such possibilities and sees dreamers and naïve believers, treasure hunters sure to be disappointed in the end. Look more closely; look from within. Look with care, and you will find that there are indeed treasures to be had.

Joy of Caring

The treasures that care offers operate in a different way. We can enjoy them whether we possess them or do not possess them. It is like deep joy: it depends on no outside circumstances and does not require success-ful results. It is not in need of people or possessions, wealth or positions or accomplishments.

We can look at great examples from the Tibetan tradition, masters like Milarepa or Longchenpa, or yogis who practiced with great intensity in more recent times. They owned nothing, but it seems they were deeply happy. We might reflect that perhaps their happiness came from finding a way of care that does not depend on 'being happy.'

In the end, we can look to the Buddha. As a prince, he possessed all that the world of his time could offer, yet he gave it all up. We might wonder, what was his motivation? What was the realization that made him so certain of his course?

We do not need to know the definitive answer to these questions. It is enough to know that when we know how to care, the way stands open. When we care, we can share what we have and appreciate what life offers. We can revel in each new impression, each new appearance. All existence can manifest as offerings of perfect beauty.

In our usual way of speaking and thinking, we say that those without material belongings or those in the grip of suffering feel great distress. This is true for all who accept the same system, the same patterns. Yet it does not take much to realize that there is another way. In each moment, we have access to the mind and the senses. We can feel and we can imagine, we can reason and we can speculate. Surely these are riches to explore, no matter our circumstances and conditions.

All of us know about the patterns that limit us and the emotionality that creeps into all our waking moments. We know about the troubles that result. Even here, however, treasures are available if we know how to look within. Once we open the door of caring, we can look gently and calmly at each new situation. We can connect fully with each point and every instant, and we can recognize that each point is unique.

Caring is the answer to our difficulties, not because it brings them to an end, but because it shows us the way to love and respect and teaches us how to make a meaningful journey through this life. Care expands in all directions. We can care for ourselves, we can care for others, and we can care for the world in which we find ourselves.

We know enough by now about being careless. It is time to go the other way.

In these times, the world is becoming more rough and raw, more intense and more tough. That is all the more reason to care, for care can free us from suffering. Care is for the rich and the poor, those at the top and those at the bottom. Suffering is universal, so care must be universal as well. When a poor person loses ten dollars, there is suffering; when a rich person loses a million dollars, there is suffering as well. These differences matter at one level, but when we care, the differences mean nothing. The rich own more, but they also have more opportunities to lose what they have. The famous enjoy certain benefits, but they also turn their happiness over to the fickle opinions of others. Everywhere obligations and duties pile up, one on top of the other.

Since there is no escape, there is no place where care does not matter.

When we care, can we solve the problems of others? We cannot say, for problems do not always have solutions. We can care with the best of intentions and still not be able to capture the care that weighs down others and release it. On the conventional level, even the Buddha did not succeed in wiping out samsara.

But we must not despair. In the end, we are simply the messengers of care, and we can follow where it leads.

Even when we do care, we may not be open to the ways that care manifests in the cosmos, the blessings that it offers. Great masters and teachers offer their care unceasingly, but we may not be able to receive it. Their compassion is boundless, but unless we learn to discover it in our own experience, we will not be able to surrender to care when it appears.

The more we understand care, the more we recognize that care is there wherever there is pain and confusion, ignorance and suffering, and the many faces of the ego. It is there in response to the roots of our ignorance; it is there as the potential to open all these illusions. When we can open to care, blessings will come. If we have questions, answers will come. If we have pain that we ourselves do not recognize, healing will come. When we ourselves care, we can receive such blessings.

The moment we care, we receive the blessings that already radiate throughout time and space. We find in our lives a new sense of unity, and we embody the peace that comes with care. We are completely free.

This is the outcome of care. We might say it is the end of the story. In this timeless story, it makes no difference what we have or do not have, or what our physical or emotional state may be. With care, body and mind, heart and head come into balance. There is no more need for emotionality, which only leads to hate and conflict. There is no more division between the fantasies and concepts of the head and the yearning of the heart. There are no competing wishes or agendas, no contradictions and miscommunications.

If we wish to care, the unity of head and heart is a good place to begin. When we bring our being into harmony, blessings can flow, and then care becomes integral to our being. There are no concerns left unanswered, no antagonisms. Care is the solvent for all problems.

How do we care when caring seems distant? We begin with the very idea of care. At first we operate only on the level of language and concepts, but that is enough to start. Gradually our obstacles turn toward harmony, and our difficulties become more subtle, releasing little by little. At the end of that journey, we graduate into caring. There is a vast knowledge available in the simple truth of caring, and little by little we can learn to access it. The language of care is universal. Knowing that, we can begin.

Caring and Wisdom

When we learn to care, care expands. Sustained by awareness, it opens fully in all directions, 360 degrees. At that point, we can start to ask questions that open new areas of investigation. Caring becomes the vehicle for the growth of wisdom. Let us see how this could happen.

We are all familiar with the thoughts and feelings and emotions that make up our mental realm. If we look closely and patiently, we see that our feelings, moods, reactions, and judgments seem to appear from nowhere. One moment we feel one way and focus our attention in a certain direction, and the next moment a new set of feelings and concerns has popped up like a bubble in the water.

Can we question these familiar patterns and sequences, gradually expanding the scope of our inquiry into unknown territories?

A bubble pops up. Suppose it expresses a feeling. Where was that feeling in the moment before it popped up?

Did it come from a specific place or location? Did it have the same form before it arrived? When it disappears, to be replaced by another bubble, where does it go? What determines how long it persists?

There is more. How do I know that the bubble—loneliness, joy, guilt, pain, excitement, fear, worry—is mine? What makes me claim ownership over it? What if I did not claim ownership? Would anything change?

These seem like fundamental questions, but perhaps we are making assumptions that also need to be questioned. When we ask where bubbles come from, are we really sure that bubbles have a 'from'? "Well, yes!" comes the answer. "Nothing arises without coming 'from' some set of circumstances and conditions." This amounts to saying that events always have a cause, and that seems reasonable. If you deny causality, you seem to be discarding the view that there is an order to our world. Anything could happen at any time, for any reason or no reason. Suddenly everything stops making sense. Only in dreams do things happen without a cause. In reality, it's a different story.

To say this another way, every single moment seems to confirm that events have a 'from' and that causality is in operation. If I open the door, that act is part of a whole series of events that unfold in sequence. We could start with my intention to go outside, which somehow gets translated into a set of complex physical reactions in my nervous system, all of which eventually ends with my reaching out my hand, turning the door handle, and pulling the door open. Each event or sequence causes the next, and each depends on the one or ones before it.

Maybe this is so, but let's keep an open mind. The aim here is to ask questions that can help us understand the suffering and frustration we all experience, so there seems to be no reason not to continue with our questions. If we care about that suffering, we may well want to do so.

Let's look more closely at the example of dreams. Suppose in a dream we drive off a road, and the car we are in starts to fall toward the ocean far below. It seems very real, and we are terrified. Then we wake up, and the whole situation vanishes. All that is left is the memory.

It might be worthwhile to trace out the sequence of events in the dream. We are driving, turning the steering wheel back and forth so that we stay on the road, and then something goes wrong. Perhaps we take a turn too quickly, and we lose control. We experience the result in all its vivid detail.

But where did any of those dream events come from? How did they arise? How do I happen to be on the road? Where is the road located? Where am I headed? How long have I been driving? At some point there are no answers to these questions. The fact (in the dream) of my being on the road, driving in a car, is part of a set of circumstances that unfold in a causal sequence, but that whole sequence is also part of the dream. If we poke at it with our questions, it turns out to be no more real than any of the rest of the dream.

When we look at this situation with caring eyes, what we recognize is the stuckness, the commitment to the truth of the bubble that has popped up and now surrounds us on all sides. Bubbles like that feel very real, and people do get lost in them. Because they offer no way out, they can take over our lives, at least till they pop of their own accord. If they don't pop, people can end up torturing themselves for a long time, because they are committed to the truth of the bubble. They can even become suicidal.

Care can be the solvent for this kind of stuckness. If we can somehow bring care into the situation, into the bubble, it dissolves our commitment to what has bubbled up. We don't need to go into the whole causal story, the whole explanation and set of perceptions that we generate to justify what we are feeling. Because we care, none of that matters.

That 'doesn't matter' can help us see that we are not bound to the emotion bubble. Look at the emotion in this way, and it dissolves. It's not so much that the bubble is real or not real, but that care does not care—not about that question. That is the wisdom—inseparable from care—that can offer us freedom.

Activating the Wisdom of Care

To apply the solvent of care, we need to educate and exercise our caring, so that it becomes strong enough to deal with any circumstances. Care can communicate positive feelings and sincerity. It finds expression in genuine loving qualities, in sympathy and compassion, in willingness and sincerity. These are not qualities we can talk ourselves into. Sophisticated arguments or clever analogies will not help. What matters is care. The more we care, the more caring will work its wonders spontaneously.

As we grow more familiar with caring, we can become models of caring, helping others to activate their own care. Gradually we may learn to come up with solutions to our pressing problems, because whenever bubbles of emotionality and negativity pop up to cloud our understanding, they will almost immediately dissolve.

It is deeply important that we learn to activate caring in this way. For all the advances in technology that this society has come up with, for all the knowledge that science, religion, and philosophy have to offer, we still face difficulties—at the personal, social, and global levels— that we do not know how to overcome. This is where caring comes in. When we hold on to our problems, when we feel them closing in on us like monsters that threaten to destroy everything we have built up, care offers a message of hope and healing. It gives us an ability to penetrate what otherwise seems profoundly solid.

In this culture, we typically rely on rationality for solutions to our problems. That is not enough. Without care, awareness based on reason and analysis becomes a dictator. It tells us what to do, it offers solutions, but it is trying to solve our bubble problems from inside the bubble. Rationality has a sharp, penetrating quality—we could even say it is diamond-like. But you cannot pop the bubble with this kind of sharpness: you cannot cut through it. Bubbles pop when the heart and soul become vulnerable. That is when the power of care to dissolve can work its magic.

Care shows us how to meet the needs of the crying child. It offers the blind a new language of perception. It lets us manifests parenthood for the world.

In ancient times, people understood that wisdom depended on the unity of heart and head, but today that understanding is rare. We know how to polish and harden the intellect till it gleams, but we do not quite know how to let the heart be vulnerable.

Yet it is the vulnerable heart that proves to be indestructible.

We might think of the mind as being like a precocious child. Able to make sense of what is going on, it knows how to reason and explain and insist. It knows how to get its way. Now, however, it is time for mind to grow up, to awaken into real wisdom. This means expanding care to others. When people care only for themselves and what they call 'mine', they have lost touch with the wisdom of care. Only when caring and wisdom teach us who we really are can we create the conditions that will let us go forward into the future with confidence and faith.

Before the Real

As far as I know, babies and very young children seldom have dreams. My theory for why this is so is that they have not yet formed the concepts and imagery out of which they can build a dream. With adults it is different. That is why we dream effortlessly, even if we do not always remember our dreams.

Dreams, as we have seen already, offer an interesting challenge to our usual view of what is real. Once we are in the dream, it seems real to us, in exactly the way that our waking experience seems real. Except in rare cases, we have no doubts about the reality of the dream we are having. The question never occurs to us.

At the same time, many dreams present images and events that are completely new to us. It is a puzzle to say where all this content comes from. On what basis do we manufacture it; out of what fabric do we weave its tales? Or is it even accurate to say that we are the authors of the dream, when it seems to come to us without our conscious control?

Similar questions come up for the mirages we might see on a hot day in the desert. With a mirage, the situation is different: we know that what we see is not real; we know that what we see as a river or a group of travelers is an interpretation we make of visual stimuli created by the sun, moisture, and other elements in the environment. Even so, the mirage continues to look real. Some animals also see mirages, and it seems that for them, the mirage appears to be completely real.

It seems that mirages vary in intensity depending on how much energy we put into them. For instance, if we are very thirsty, the mirage of a river seems especially vivid. If we run toward the mirage, it grows more vivid as well. I am sure science has something to say about this.

Then there is the example of an echo that comes back to you when you shout or chant in a canyon. Everyone knows this phenomenon, which seems to work best with simple sounds such as HA or O or E. Sometimes echoes can bounce back and forth, so that we hear the same sound many times.

Finally, there are rainbows. Here the scientific explanation is very clear and direct, but the explanation has no impact at all on how we see the rainbow. Some rainbows are fuzzy, almost invisible, while others are sharp and clear—as clear as the objects around them.

All these examples represent very ordinary circumstances and situations. If we imagine encountering them for the first time, we might find them mysterious, but we all learn about them growing up, and in some ways we take them for granted.

Similarly, it is easy enough to recognize that the way we make sense of the world depends on the labels we assign our different perceptions. I see what I have been conditioned to see or expect to see. If something out of the ordinary appears, I may not even notice, because my immediate reaction is to see it as an example of something I already know about. For instance, if I am used to passing by a restaurant every day, it might be days or weeks before I realize that it has changed ownership and is serving a different cuisine.

All this is also quite clear and predictable. Less clear, however, is the role that mind plays in this activity of making sense out of experience. Where do the labels I apply come from? It seems safe to say that they originate with the mind. But mind is also active at a later stage, after there has been an act of perception, for it is mind that decides which label fits the perception. It seems that mind plays a dual role, both supplying the label and applying the label. If mind did not play both roles—mind giving feedback to mind—there could be no knowing, no definitions, and no interpretations.

These two functions of mind seem intimately related. The mind tells me something, and I repeat it back. I download mind's data and upload the response. It is like one body with two heads. The subject applies a label to the object, and the object feeds that same label back to the subject.

What we are really talking about is an act of recognition. We find what we are searching for, because that is how we have been taught to search. Knowledge goes *from* the mind *to* the mind, in a loop that repeats itself.

All this may be true for perception, but what about before perception? Is perception just another bubble, popping up without explanation? On one level, the answer is no, since I will not perceive a tree before me if there is no tree there. In that sense the tree is the cause of the perception.

But that is not the level we are looking at. We are interested in the workings of the mind. A situation arises in which a tree is before me. How does it happen that I perceive it? Here we have to look more sensitively. Is there a knowing capacity before the perception, before the bubble pops into place?

If we look, we might find such a 'before'. It is like the time of dawn before the sun actually arises, a time when a glimmer of light has begun to appear. It might not even be light, but a certain feeling that light is on the horizon. We could think of this as the 'from' of perception.

Of course, the light before sunrise is only an analogy. The point is to suggest the possibility of a knowing before perception, before an object has been identified and the bubble appears. We might say that the perception is complete when the object is perceived; for instance, when the rays of the rising sun bounce off a window or a mountain range. But what comes before?

Before sunrise, there is light. Such light is not different from light after the sun has fully risen, any more than the water at the ocean shore differs in its wetness from the water on the high seas. In the same way, if mind is the source of the knowing before perception that makes perception possible, that knowing will not be different from the knowing that comes after the bubble is in place, the knowing that applies labels and names identities, including the identities 'I' or 'me' or 'mine'. When we specify experience, both aspects of knowing operate, mind talking to mind. It is like the reflection of the moon in a hundred different ponds: a hundred images, each a separate perception, but only one moon.

Mind is thus the active party, both before and after. 'Before', it projects a knowing outward, but if that is all, the act of knowing remains incomplete. Only when the object has been identified does mind's activity reach its goal. At that point, the mission has been accomplished. Knowledge has shifted from one phase to another, like a boat crossing a river.

By identifying these two aspects of the mind's activity, we come across a new question. What happens between the initial knowing impulse—the light before dawn—

and the completed act of knowing? As labels and patterns of language start to be applied, there must be transitions. In those transitions, are there gaps? Are there blank spaces? Could we discover such gaps through our own inner inquiry?

Suppose for now that there are such gaps, moments of uncertainty or not knowing 'built in' to the act of knowing. We can say that these blank spaces are a part of the knowing—they would not be there without it—but they are also a kind of not knowing. We could think of them as shadows cast by the light of knowing, or like the dark matter that is said to pervade the universe, but for now is completely unknowable. As with dark matter, we can imagine that while we cannot know the gaps, we could investigate a ratio between the knowing that perceives and identifies and the unknowing that makes up the gaps.

The Many Moons of Mind

These may seem like rather unusual ideas. They suggest possibilities that no one ordinarily recognizes. But if we take them seriously, they raise the possibility there is a vast ignorance at the heart of our ordinary understanding of mind. Science, philosophy, and psychology all do their best to track down and investigate mind's operations, each in its own way. But if there are truly unknown operations occurring in the blank spaces between mind's dialogue with mind, such efforts are doomed. All our labels and theories are missing something truly fundamental.

Someone might say, "Surely this is wrong! Yes, our standard knowledge of mind is incomplete, but that doesn't mean it leaves out something essential. After all, we make wonderful discoveries about mind all the time."

There may be something to this, but there are reasons to wonder. No one has ever seen or touched the mind. Science has no way to detect it. The very idea of mind arises on the basis of feedback from the operation of the senses, the body's reactivity, and various forms of physical energy. Mind reaches out to know the world, but when we try to turn that operation around and know the mind that knows, we have nothing to go on but mind's reflections. We can look at the inputs to mind and the outputs of mind; we can identify mind's expressions and the impressions it receives, but none of that brings us any closer to mind itself.

Of course, we all use the label 'mind' to identify the agent at the center of all our knowing operations. But we cannot really say what the label is pointing to. When we respond to an input or assign a name or identity, we confidently say that it is 'mind' that does all this. Yet the basis for applying this label seems shaky. Who is it that responds? Where does the response take place? How does it happen? We don't have a clue.

This not-knowing has some powerful consequences. If we do not know the nature of mind, how solid is any of the knowledge we collect? Mind labels and identifies and reacts, and it projects its knowing capacity out into the world. It gives us 'yes' and 'no' and right and wrong. But whatever inputs mind receives and whatever outputs it generates will reflect mind itself, just as an echo reflects the original sound. The knowledge mind produces will repeat patterns that the mind imposes, patterns that have been cast in advance. Our ways of knowing and what it is they know are caught in a loop.

It is a little like the theory of the Big Bang as the origin of the universe. We can trace back everything that happens to the instant immediately after the Big Bang, and we can investigate with ever greater specificity how events have unfolded from that point. But the Big Bang itself is just the label for a mystery. We cannot observe it or point to it. We cannot locate it in space or time because it is the origin of space and time. It is beyond the reach of our search engines.

If mind itself is mysterious—an unknown Big Bang—we are walking each and every moment on shaky ground. All our knowledge depends on mind. The questions I ask come from mind; the answers I receive are presented by mind; the data I collect and the methods I use to collect it also depend on the operations of mind. We take those operations for granted, but if we cannot trace them to their source, if we cannot even identify their source, our confidence in what we know—all of what we know—seems misplaced.

Imagine that someone is an expert at playing chess. They have studied extensively the record of past games, they know how each opening unfolds, and they have memorized all possible end games. Yet none of that knowledge tells us anything about the game of chess itself. Who made the rules that every player must follow? How did they evolve? That is a different field of knowledge entirely. Knowing how to follow the rules and developing expertise in how to operate within the rules has nothing to do with knowing how the rules themselves were set up.

In the same way, we all know a great deal about how to operate with the knowledge-rules that mind has established. We cannot say that we know everything, because the field of samsara is vast. It includes whole civilizations, all possible disciplines of study, countless inventions, and endless moments in the flow of history. Even the laws governing causality and the natural world, along with the flow of time from past to present to future fit within this structure. Yet even if we could expand exponentially our knowledge of this structure—the regime that mind has set up, the game whose rules we play by—we would not have learned any more about how the regime came into being or who is responsible.

It is just at that point that we introduce mind as the one in charge. But that is just a label. Who is this 'mind', the boss responsible for the whole operation? Who is the producer, the sponsor? It seems impossible to give answers to these questions using the knowledge that mind makes available. Yet what other choice is there?

We can come at these same difficulties from other directions. Consider our knowledge of the physical world. The objects we encounter—earth, trees, bodies—all have their own shape and form. They have certain distinguishing characteristics or marks that make them what they are. Each of these marks or shapes is available to investigate. Looking at a circle, I can mark out 30 degrees or 90 degrees or 270 degrees. I can measure its circumference. I can determine whether it exists in two dimensions (a circle) or three dimensions (a sphere). In principle, I can look at all possible dimensions—an infinite number of dimensions.

To carry out this kind of investigation, I rely on locating particular points in time and space. Points let me trace out derivation and directionality. They also let me establish ratios—the relation of one set of points to another. On the basis of ratios, I can build up the known world: not just solid things, but human structures such as buildings designed by architects, works of art such as sculptures and paintings, and the creative rhythms of music. Ratios allow for feedback, letting us distinguish one set of shapes and forms from another.

We do not usually ask what makes all these forms and ratios possible, but an answer is available. It is space that manifests all these shapes and forms. Without space, where would they appear?

Now, however, we have arrived at the same kind of difficulty we encountered when we looked at mind. Space itself does not seem to be detectable by the ways of knowing we apply to objects that appear *within* space. We know how to identify top and bottom, large and small, straight and curved. We can specify direction and movement, even 'is' and 'is not'. But none of these characteristics apply to space. Space allows manifestation, but it does not itself manifest.

We said before that without mind, there could be no consciousness or thoughts, no cognition, no sense experience, no feelings or emotions, and no sense of identity; yet mind itself is nowhere to be found. Space has an identical relationship to what appears in space: indispensable but also inaccessible.

Ripples in Space and Time

We could think of the relation between space and appearance as being like the relation between the water in a lake and the ripples or waves that pass through the lake. When it comes to the ripples, we can expand our knowledge indefinitely. Suppose we plant a tree and trace its growth over thirty years. Think of that as a ripple in space. At any moment we can measure the tree's height and circumference and describe in detail its appearance. We can quantify what is happening, and we can appreciate aesthetically what cannot be quantified. In the same way we can plot sunrise and sunset and measure out the days and years and decades; we can separate out the past from the future. At any point, we can stop and say, "That's it. That's how it is."

These are all ripples, and we can mark them out. Sometimes our marks seem arbitrary; for instance, if we put out cultured milk, at some point it will turn into yogurt, but it is difficult to identify the precise point at which that happens. In the same way, a baby turns into an adult, and gradually through the years the signs of aging appear: wrinkles, white hair, aches and pains. The transitions are gradual, and the labels we apply to separate one phase from another cannot be fully justified. Yet we depend on such clearly defined distinctions in countless ways.

We do the same thing with time. One moment flows into the next in a dynamic rhythm, but we abstract out from that flow a set of markers: the hours on a sundial, the minutes on a clock, the end of spring and the beginning of summer. We engage the ripples of appearance within space *and* time through abstractions that name and give specific characteristics to what manifests in a more fluid and constantly changing way.

Let us return now to mind, the mysterious actor, and the role it plays in our knowledge. Mind makes available the range of concepts. It cooperates with language to gain agreement, so that one word means the same thing to different people. It gives us a general sense of good and bad, right and wrong, subjective and objective. Concepts and labels proliferate in a process that accelerates over time: by some estimates, there are now over a million words in the English language. All this is problematic, for in our labeling we rely on the principles of abstraction. We give the labels we apply and the categories they produce priority over the actual appearances that manifest in space.

By using concepts and labels to point out and pin down the ripples of appearance, mind creates a new set of blank spaces in our body of knowledge. Milk becomes yogurt, but what can we say of the transition? The baby becomes a child: just when does that happen? Ice melts into water: all at once or bit by bit? We clean a room, but just how clean is clean? Using the ways of knowing the mind provides, we lose track of the immediacy of what we experience. The result is that gaps arise. Because we make use of frozen concepts, we have to account for the transitions between them. Another gap, another mystery—one we are so familiar with that we almost never notice it in operation.

We are left with our known unknowns and our unknown unknowns. Usually we focus on the knowns and ignore the unknowns. We name what is real, and we ignore the gap between the name and what it names, just as we ignore the gap between the knowledge that lets us identify and the knowledge before identity comes to be.

Still, we are not trapped for all time in such unknowns. We human beings possess curiosity. We are ready to ask where something comes from, what it means, or how it works. Our desire to know motivates and energizes us. We use the mind to ask, and mind feeds back whatever knowledge is available, but we know that what has been established will not always be good enough. That is what makes us curious.

In the act of being curious, what has been settled becomes unsettled. There are no rules, no certainty, and no fixed place at which to arrive. We know that we do not know. We know that our cognition is inadequate, so we must continue. Could this be a way into the gaps?

Beyond Limits

Light travels in waves. It radiates outward until it reaches some barrier or limit and is reflected back toward its source. The limit becomes a puzzle for light, a puzzle to solve, a kind of reflection.

This is what happens when we look in a mirror and our image is reflected back to us.

That is only one example. Our fingers strike the keyboard, and images of letters are reflected onto the computer screen. There are only a few dozen keys on the keyboard, but they can manifest an infinity of words that all reflect the concepts and language the mind makes available. The words that appear on the screen can be printed out on paper: more reflections, more ways that our limits will feed back what has been projected. It is like casting someone in a play to deliver the lines of the script, or casting an image in clay to give expression to the sculptor's intent. Whatever appears automatically has a role to play and duties to perform.

Mind, our partner, can manifest such interactions across many different media. Mind projects, and what it projects is fed back to it duplicated or modified. Depending on concepts and labels, drawing on language, mind offers up thoughts and questions; it speculates, and it creates puzzles.

We respond to what mind transmits, offering our own feedback. First, we download what is transmitted, then we acknowledge receipt, and then we process it and send it back. We respond to what mind knows, giving it our own expression. We accept the position of the subject, and from that position we feed back what has been projected. We ourselves, together with what appears to us, could be seen as mind's echoes.

All this is not so difficult to describe, but again and again we come up against the same mystery: the mystery of the 'before' and the 'between'; the mystery of the gaps. The sun shines, but how does the sun appear? The egg hatches, but where did the egg come from?

We experience joy or suffering, but how do such feelings originate?

Within the regime, we have answers to give. We say, "I'm unhappy because somebody criticized me." The story is complete: I hear what has been said, interpret it, and react in predictable ways. First there is a vague cloudiness, then a feeling, then a judgment and response. I heard what I heard, and I know the person meant it. A sequence of unfolding factors eventually hits me, almost like a physical blow or a pungent smell. Inevitably, I react.

None of this, however, tells us anything about the 'between' or the 'before.' There is light before dawn: how does it arise? We cognize appearance, but what about the first stirring of awareness, before cognition? The immediate instant pops up like a bubble, but we cannot trace its origins.

This is not some conceptual point to debate and speculate over; it points to something with an enormous impact on our well-being. Our ways of reacting, and the ignorance out of which they emerge, color every moment of our lives. When something negative arises out of an unknown 'before,' we react with anger or shock or defensiveness.

> *How could this bad thing happen to me? Why am I the victim?*

We may fall into depression or confusion, or perhaps defensive pride or insecurity. The exact flavor does not matter. The patterns are the same.

Think about it. Each moment, each new happening is its own bubble. Whatever we name, whatever we perceive, whatever the content—another bubble. What comes before the bubble? Naming the causes and conditions is not enough, because they are a part of the bubble. We are looking for a different 'before', a 'before' of the gaps, and we explore across unknown 'betweens'. Could such an exploration be an antidote to our difficulties, our negativities? Could we see before seeing, know between knowing?

We do not have to understand the naming of such possibilities as some kind of new theory. We do not have to accept it all. But perhaps such named possibilities can make us wonder; perhaps they can encourage us to look within the immediacy of our experience, look at a different level. Would such an inquiry affect the inner atmosphere in which we live and breathe? Would it awaken our appreciation for the creative power of mind? Could it turn that creativity in new directions?

If we no longer had to follow the rules that everyone accepts, if we no longer stamped each perception with the label 'real', what would become of our problems? Would they still be there in the same way, or would they dissolve? Could we find an easy entry into ease?

We may say that we don't know how to question in this way, and perhaps this is true, because everything we learn makes it seem impossible. But we do not have to try to do what seems beyond our capacities. We can start simply by facing our difficulties, the emotions that overwhelm us, the shadows that fall across our lives. When we experience them fully, we can look for their origins, for the place 'beyond' or 'between'.

It does not require penetrating insight. We simply need to *embody* the possibility of knowing differently. Perhaps what erupts into our lives lacks the substance the mind assigns to it. Perhaps it is a magical display, a creation that need not bind us.

Different religious traditions speak of ways we humans can free ourselves from samsara, even if they do not use that term. They say that we can find our way to heaven, or nirvana, or enlightenment, or union with God, or a realm of perfect beauty. These are worthwhile goals. We might say that they are gateways into a beyond that is not really beyond.

What we are describing here, however, offers another way. We can accept samsara as it is, for it does not have the power over us that we think it does. Once we understand more about how samsara manifests, how it is created, we see that there is no need to go anywhere else. We see how the rules we follow have been set up, and we see how our reactions arise in perfect obedience to this structure. At that point, each new difficulty loses its hold over us. It is a little like waking up within a nightmare: we see what is happening, but we also see that it is not real in the way it claims to be. We gain the confidence to face any difficulty.

All this may not make much sense if we accept the claims of materialist ways of thinking, which uphold this physical realm as the one and only reality. In that way of seeing, we have no choices, no other ways of knowing. Questions about freedom and inner joy remain only as puzzles.

Yet we could imagine that Western science examined the basis of its materialist paradigm, and took a different turn: that it began to explore the possibility of a spiritual dimension within our lived reality. It would not be that difficult to set such an inquiry into motion, and it might lead in interesting ways to deeper insights. It might lead us into the 'before' and the 'between' of what appears—into the unknowns. At that time, the ideas explored here might prove helpful.

Traditions that recognize realms beyond our ordinary existence—heavens filled with deities or angels, or other divine abodes—find it difficult to communicate with those who reject such an understanding. Perhaps seeing appearance as a beautiful, powerful, but baseless creation could help. Perhaps knowledge that penetrated to this level could make a real dialogue possible.

We will find out only if we can creatively embody such possibilities. In the distant past—in ancient Greece, among the Buddhist lands of Asia, or in Egypt—such ways of seeing may have been more widely known. It is hard to say. What we do know is that the knowledge available today is sufficient to allow dialogue to flourish. Science could engage the Mantrayana, psychology could interact with the study of how language arises within us, reason could admit other possibilities for knowing. Every discipline, every tradition, has its own way of understanding creation. There are countless opportunities for new ways of knowing to arise.

Caring from the Heart

Here is some parting advice: No matter what, don't be a traitor to yourself.

Do not trade your happiness away; do not sell yourself out in exchange for anxiety, resentment, addiction, and loneliness.

Promise yourself now: *From here on out, to the best of my ability, I will take care of myself, body and mind, emotions and perceptions. From here on out, I will make the most of my journey.*

We thought we wanted to be distracted from our troubled thoughts; we thought we wanted to chase our desires and run from our fears. But none of us wanted the woeful outcomes we can see in ourselves and our loved ones.

These patterns are hypnotic and deceptive. This set-up has been reinforced by our own friends and family, colleagues and coworkers—it has been endorsed by the underlying assumptions of every human culture, of every institution. We are all in the same trap.

Whenever we tell ourselves, "You are terrible"; whenever we decide, "I can't help myself"; we bow our heads and accept our conditioning. Our minds have an astonishing power to shape our reality, depending on the story they endorse. When we endorse unkindness and resentment—when we treat caring as something we have to hoard, or when we decide real caring is just an illusion—we head deeper into a mind-imposed hypnosis.

We are caught—caught in habit's crocodile jaws.

When we understand this dynamic, though, we find ourselves in a stronger position. We may even be able to negotiate with these powerful forces and bring them over to our side. We can work out a new deal with our minds.

> *Why did I do this to myself?*
>
> *Because I had no choice. The circumstances were set up. The deck was stacked against me from the start.*
>
> *Now I willingly perpetuate the trick. I've become a trickster, too!*
>
> *I tricked myself.*

I really believed that my only chance at happiness was to play out these patterns. I fell for it! The obsession, the disillusionment, just leads to guilt.

When I try to slip away from the consequences, I make more patterns. Those patterns manifest misery, too. Not just for me! My parents had patterns, a gloomy inheritance. Is this going to be my legacy?

I don't want that for myself or anyone else.

But even now those tricky habits persist! They tell me I shouldn't enter negotiations with myself, shouldn't even try! "I am what I am," they say. "I have a strong sense of self! This is my identity! Changing is bad, it's dangerous! I AM IN IT NOW. Don't try to escape."

… That's my jailor talking.

I really have been betrayed. I've lost it all. I have nothing left to lose!

I won't be tricked anymore.

A good financial advisor can warn us if we are in danger of losing our money. He or she can let us know that we are making a bad investment and help us find an alternative.

When it comes to protecting our inner well-being and our potentials—when it comes to protecting our power to help ourselves and others—we have few such advisors, and we may feel there are no alternatives.

But they do exist. With practice and a little guidance, we can discover them for ourselves and confirm their reality with certainty.

I hope that this book has begun to introduce some practices and methods that can help us, but it only scratches the surface. There is much more we can learn. We can develop our own approach through the careful study of our own minds. Where are the snares, the traps of the over-mastered mind? What signals can we detect to let us know a trap is there before it snaps shut?

We need to put aside our doubts and regrets and make a determined commitment to realization. For these patterns are powerful. They've been with us a long time; they're in our blood, our bones, and they overtake us at a moment's notice. The agents of these patterns are woven into our thoughts, secretly selling us out. Separating them out so we can see them more clearly is definitely a challenge.

It seems we are deeply entangled with the patterns keeping us prisoner. But we can still act, still negotiate.

Looking closely, we can discover how these painful experiences take root. We can examine their earliest appearances. We can study how they occur, how we came to be caught up, and how this initial self-betrayal culminates in the patterns we call 'behavior.'

> *I don't want to treat myself that way, not anymore. I can't take it lightly. I need to find my backbone, get methods and techniques to help me. I must believe in myself and trust that there is a way forward.*

> *Can I catch these inner betrayers in the act? Can I learn to identify when I've become hypnotized again? I've got to try, for the sake of everyone who's in the same trouble as me!*

Our pathway starts with recognition. It opens up when we allow ourselves to feel genuine sympathy and empathy, for ourselves and others. When sympathy and empathy are real and alive within us, they become a powerful motivation to care.

Given this encouragement, caring can emerge effortlessly, rising up from deep inside to permeate all we are, all we do. This quality of caring, at its heart, is indestructible.

> *I think I need to care. We can't afford to just let this go. It's unbearable—unthinkable. No one cares; you can see it on the streets, you can feel it even in places where everything looks OK on the outside. Inside, we're all messed up, we're all trapped.*

> *Is there anyone who isn't trapped? Can we find out? Is there someone out there who doesn't lose*

their heart and head again and again, someone who takes care of their spirit? People like that might be models. Can we reproduce their results?

"You're exaggerating. Not everybody is in this trouble. We don't need models for some different way. It's not that bad. Anyway, we can't get out."

You can say things like that, but I know the truth now: you're bluffing.

All the world is lonely. All of us have been taught to seek these short-term solutions. We can drown ourselves in sensation, but eventually every one of our pleasures disappears. We end up worse off than we were before.

When we keep trying to get by with fake care, fake comfort, over time our light falters; darkness comes. And the ripples of the rhythms of our basic impermanence? They go on and on.

We need alternatives, antidotes. I've tasted real peace now. If I make a careful study of caring, I'll get more confidence in the feeling of that positivity. It will become part of me: my soul will be in the right place.

When heart and head, soul and spirit are working together, we have a sturdy basis for happiness. Then, the parts of us that used to work against us, parts of that self-betraying system, can actually become allies. Even our ancient tendency to identify patterns can contribute in a deep and meaningful way to wisdom, as it shows us how to interpret history, how to detect subtle clues in advance that will help keep us out of our habitual traps.

> *An early-warning system would be nice... I usually don't notice I've been kidnapped again until it's too late.*

> *The thing is, I have these memories and associations. They are so familiar, I'm tempted to do things my usual way. In the past, I didn't notice how I slipped back into the chains. I almost didn't want to know about the attempted kidnapping...!*

Even the knowledgeable among us—even those we sometimes call 'masters'—can be re-captured. Since it happens all the time, we might reason that it is pointless to try to protect our inner freedom. But reason is not our best friend in this case.

Reason is very easily co-opted by our kidnappers. Reason readily becomes *reasons*, excuses for leaving things the same. If we want to prevent these painful circumstances from happening again, we need to provide ourselves with real solutions, not excuses.

We don't want to give any more ammunition to these kidnappers.

> *I'm willing—I want to try—but I need a method.*

When we take the path of caring, we have a truly excellent method, one we can follow no matter how we feel at that moment, and no matter what we perceive the level of our understanding to be. In caring, we:

1. Pay close attention, inside and out.

2. Look for common ground, ready to share our sympathy.

3. Treat caring as a precious vehicle, a reliable source of support, made stronger by our awareness.

We may not be perfect, but we keep on learning: we can be grateful for the opportunities our experiences bring us, even pain. Our misfortunes can become a source of knowledge, a rich soil in which better experiences will grow. Having been through so much, we value our peace of mind.

> *I've finally gotten to the point where I don't want to hurt myself anymore. It's taken time to learn, but I'm grateful. I think this realization may be very important.*

> *I wish my family and friends knew what I'm learning. It's hard to explain sometimes. There must be a way to communicate the value. I won't give up until I find it.*

> *I will learn.*

> *I will understand.*

Epilogue

I'll get out of the maze.

I will share the way out with others.

The knowledge we're gaining helps us look at our experience very differently. The ocean ripples catch the light now: our world's dramas can be true *plays*, with a special beauty and interest we couldn't see before.

When we learn to relate to our experience in this way, we gain access to a wisdom that is not found in books. We begin to recognize the way the shapes and forms of our experience arise, play out, and disappear—and we learn how to make the most out of these changes.

We can learn through these transitions, gaining wisdom from the ocean's moving currents. Now we can be grateful even to the parts of ourselves that collaborated in our suffering.

> *I can transform even you... I'll transform you*
> *into wisdom. When your patterns are detoxified,*
> *that poison could become nectar.*

Our models, our greatest examples, may have learned wisdom this way. Following their lead, we may be able to experience a total transformation, a complete graduation from these ancient, painful patterns.

Admittedly, it's a big task! It will take patience, generosity of spirit, self-forgiveness, and deep awareness. We will need to be willing to make a close study of our own journey, willing to bear witness to our own learning process, so that we can help others develop as we do, step by step.

At the very least, if we understand and appreciate the power of caring in our bones, we can become messengers, sharing with others what has brought us to this place, what has taught us the great importance of caring.

One day, your family and friends might say: "There's something different about you these days. You seem wiser and kinder. What happened? How did you change?"

You can tell them:

> *I practiced caring awareness and did my best to love myself. When I was able to do that, I discovered goodness in myself that I wanted to protect. Then I began to notice that same goodness in others.*
>
> *I learned through my own imperfections: that is how I got this knowledge.*

Knowing to Care

We have been given a precious human life, and how we live it in relation to those around us is important. Our families, friends, communities large and small, and all sentient beings—both known and unknown to us—need us to be available, offering the best we have in our daily lives. How can we do this? The answers to that question are complex and involve many elements, some of which we have dscussed in the chapters of this book.

We have explored caring from several angles. We have acknowledged what the mind does well—naming and structuring our experiences—but we have also noticed the ways that the operations of mind and language keep us trapped in suffering. We have learned that language is *mind work*, creating a closed loop that we must interrupt if we are to break through to deeper caring.

We have explored exercises to broaden our understanding of why caring matters, and we may have experienced moments of the spaciousness of deep caring as we practiced. In doing so, we may have recognized that we want more of that feeling. We have thus brought home a souvenir of sorts of our travels into realms of caring—a reminder, if not yet the full expression of caring's real potentials.

We have begun to see that while we can learn methods and techniques to break through to deep caring, even when we perform these methods skillfully, we may still be caught in mind's regime. In fact, we have been trapped this way for a very long time. The mind thinks it knows what to do, but it cannot notice what language cannot express.

We have explored what it takes to experience the wisdom of caring. We have discovered that we have the ability to gain an awareness of caring before the mind takes over, like an awareness of light before dawn breaks. We have learned that relaxing before thoughts arise and intentionally holding caring can help open the way to this new possibility. We have learned that we can experience a dynamic knowledge and genuine caring that is liberating. And we have begun to see that caring is real, and not just a concept.

We may even have sensed that caring has a specific quality all its own, a quality we can experience directly; and thus, with practice, we can learn to embody caring and wisdom ourselves.

Going in a new direction is not always easy, even when we trust that the destination is a good one, for we are not familiar with the road to that new way of being. For this reason, we need to be sure that our caring journey begins with caring for ourselves, so that we can support ourselves as we learn.

There are many elements to good self-care that range from basic care of the body and attention to resources, to making careful choices that enrich our lives and build character.

We can maintain a stable body through a healthy diet, restful sleep, and the ways we nurture and use our body's energy. This provides a base from which we can engage in our daily activities. We can take care of our mind by learning to understand how it works, treasuring its knowledge, and growing in wisdom. We want to be able to use our minds without distractions, and without being overwhelmed by the thinking of others or by our own negativity. Using the mind's amazing capacity to learn is also important, especially when it comes to learning ways to avoid wasting time and energy. Engaging in vigorous contemplation is essential, as contemplation can help us be well-grounded as we learn to manifest wise mind, joyful energy and deep patience. Then we are able to consciously serve and involve ourselves with others.

How we manage our resources also affects our physical and mental well-being. It is important to be prudent in choosing what we will own; minimizing our possessions allows us to be free of debt. Purchasing thoughtfully and looking after what we purchase will allow our things will serve us well for a long time. Learning how to manage our financial resources is likewise important, so that we have funds available when they are needed for whatever life brings. When we do this, we also gain the freedom to practice generosity as an act of caring.

A commitment to growing in wisdom is another aspect of taking care of ourselves. Reading and studying encourage us to broaden our thinking and discover novel approaches to our experience. Conversations with others about what we are learning can help foster new ways of thinking. Time spent with others in meaningful activity develops a practical wisdom that allows us to be healthier, both emotionally and physically. We need to remember to celebrate life and appreciate the present, remembering that the present is all we have. The wisdom that grows from experience and learning will influence the amount of caring we can feel and demonstrate in our daily lives.

Another area for our attention is our gestures toward other beings: the words we use, our facial expressions, and our actions throughout the day. We can cultivate sweetness in our attitude and remain calm and polite in all our interactions. We can learn to take the time to be kind to all the beings we encounter in our daily journeys.

Improving our character is an additional area to study and practice. When we take responsibility for how our character develops, we can more clearly recognize that our choices influence who we become. Qualities that are hallmarks of a good character include patience, endurance, tolerance and kindness.

• Patience with ourselves and others allows us to take the time to be present even when we are tired or encountering obstacles. It helps us to slow down and be open to what is really happening, rather than making assumptions that lead to uncaring responses.

• Endurance encompasses both physical and emotional resources. When we wish to show caring to another, we may need to persist beyond what we had expected. Caring is not always easy, and can require resources we did not know we had and did not plan on using. But if we are to demonstrate true caring, we must be willing to finish what we have begun.

• Showing tolerance towards others as a way of caring suggests the need to allow our thinking to broaden beyond what we have considered 'correct' or 'acceptable.' There are many ways of thinking and being that can lead to a good journey through this life, and honestly appreciating that variety can be a caring gesture toward someone whose path is different from ours.

• Kindness might seem to be a small or simple thing, but in fact it is one of the most important attitudes we can develop. When we approach other beings with kindness, we carry an intention to be caring and also to do no harm. With kind gestures, we acknowledge what is precious in all of us and celebrate the journeys we take. We do not thrive without kindness in our lives.

No one is perfect in their cultivation of the qualities described above. But it is important to know how to take care of ourselves in many ways in order to live a more meaningful life. Reminding ourselves that we are worthy of care helps us develop a sense of our potentials and allows us to participate fully in what life brings. Our memories of joys and successes can become virtues, and we can live without regret.

We need to remember that at a fundamental level, all lives are precious. When we can remind ourselves of the innate value of all beings, including ourselves, we can more fully act in ways that express caring.

We can choose to start each new day, each new journey, and each new life with the continuity of the wisdom and compassion gained in the past. Doing this helps us avoid getting caught up in the distractions of life that lead us to be overwhelmed and take away our joy. When it is practiced steadfastly, continuity of caring becomes one of our most precious resources.

When we consider how our individual efforts to live a wholesome life affect us and those we know, we must also recognize that our efforts have a broader importance. Who we are every day directly impacts those with whom we are in contact, but this is not the end of the story. Our influence continues to expand beyond our circle of acquaintances, because how we act affects how others act. Our actions reverberate, the ripples of our activity spreading outward from the individual choices we make each day. And our own choices go on to interact in complex ways with the choices others are making, in that we can decide how to respond to what comes to us from others.

If we wish to live up to our real potentials, we will want to act in ways that nourish and benefit all sentient beings. We will want to continue to develop our wisdom, and to manifest it in what we say, how we think, the ways we interact with others, and the ways we use our resources. We will want to demonstrate joyfulness in every circumstance, and to manifest loving-kindness as a way of life.

As we do this, it is good to remember that we teach by example. Among our peers we can serve as a model of how to live more caringly; it is important that we do so in a patient, thoughtful, and detailed way, so that our experience can be truly useful to others. As we age, we develop more depth to our understanding, and we can share the insights we have gathered over a lifetime. But we can also benefit from the wisdom of those younger than ourselves.

What matters most is that we communicate as effectively as we can the message that we can be free of suffering. We will do this when we understand what treasures lie hidden with our own minds.

In addition to sharing the wisdom we have gained in our present moment, we will wish to transmit what we have learned for the benefit of those who will follow us, so that beings in the future may also experience joy, gain the ability to care and be cared for, and uncover a deep appreciation of their lives. Our willingness to share wisdom is a powerful way to care—for ourselves, our families, our friendships, our communities, and the world.

In our interactions with others, we may serve as advisors, directors, or leaders. It is important to demonstrate sincerity and authenticity in our behavior and our communication if we are to inspire trust. In these roles, it is our responsibility to act in ways that are unselfish and that build a healthy and sustainable future. We must work cooperatively and share our knowledge if our actions are to be virtuous and successful.

As leaders, we must learn to develop a vision that is clear, balanced, and well-founded, so that others can share it and participate in making it manifest. When those who work together are inspired by such a broad, deep, and well-developed vision, they trust one other and feel secure and strong in their work.

We have a chance to live in a world where caring extends beyond caring 'about' or caring 'for,' to caring with a higher purpose. The path to that world runs through each of us, and we each make daily choices either to stay on the path or to wander away.

And so we come full circle to what may have led you to open this book: our deep desire to break the cycle of our own suffering. We are now faced with the challenge of deciding whether to continue relying on the mind's regime, or to voluntarily step into a new way of being, in which caring is inseparable from awareness.

We have gained the knowledge we need, but do we have the will to apply what we have learned, to embody care in our thoughts, gestures, expressions, and actions?

A crossroads lies ahead. What way will you choose?

A Life Devoted to Dharma Activity

Tarthang Tulku, also known as
Kunga Gellek Yeshe Dorje,
was born in Golok, Eastern Tibet, in 1935.

Thoroughly trained by traditional masters, he went into exile in 1958. After a short stay at the Young Lamas Home School in Dalhousie, he was asked by H.H. Dudjom Rinpoche to represent the Nyingma School at Sanskrit University in Varanasi. There he established Dharma Mudranalaya to print Tibetan Buddhist texts. In 1968 he left India for the United States, becoming the first Nyingma lama in America.

In 1969, Rinpoche founded the Tibetan Nyingma Meditation Center (TNMC), a California corporation sole, as the nucleus of his activities.

He established Padma Ling as a residential center, and in 1972–73 founded the Nyingma Institute, where he taught publicly until 1978. During these years he published the first of his 34 books in English to aid students in their study. He also founded the Tibetan Aid Project to support Tibetans in exile; Dharma Press and Dharma Publishing, which have now printed and produced hundreds of art reproductions and more than 130 books in Western languages; Nyingma Centers, to guide the growth of four international centers; and Odiyan Country Center, a mandala of temples, stupas, and libraries, including Vajra Temp Cintamani Temple, the Enlight ment Stupa, and Vairocana G den; Ratna Ling Retreat Cen established in 2004 as an adjunc Odiyan, offers retreats to the g eral public.

In 1981, Rinpoche published *Nyingma Edition of the Tibe Buddhist Canon* in 120 atlas-si volumes, followed by an eig volume Catalogue and Biblio phy. The Yeshe De Text Proj founded in 1983, produced G *Treasures of Ancient Teachings* 641 volumes, and has printed distributed to the Tibetan cc munity over five million boc including five versions of Kanjur and three versions of Tanjur. In its latest edition, Yeshe De Kanjur is the most cc prehensive collection ever asse bled, and includes 12 historica significant karchags, or catalogu Yeshe De is currently produc the most rare and comprehens collection of Nyingma Tantras e compiled, in 150 volumes.

In 1989 Rinpoche founded Nyingma Monlam Chen (World Peace Ceremony) in Bc Gaya, where 8–10,000 lan monks, and nuns gather annua He also provided seed money tiate the Kagyu, Sakya and Gelug onlams. Since 1989, 5 million red books, 3.25 million sacred art ages, and 176,250 prayer wheels ve been distributed to more than 00 Dharma centers in India, pal, Bhutan and Tibet. A total 66,285 copies of the precious 00-line Prajnaparamita includ- this year's offering to the 2017 nlam of 414 engraved granite ques in Sanskrit, Tibetan and glish, 100 decorative victory ners and six important editions large poti format have been of- ed to the Sangha. Other offer- s for Bodh Gaya include six ter lamp houses, 152 prayer eels, 158 golden lhantsa and etan Prajnaparamita plaques, port towards the restoration Mahabodhi Temple spire, beautification, and year-round erings of butterlamps.

2002 he founded the Light of ddhadharma Foundation to port annual Tipitaka Chant- Ceremonies by the Theravadin gha, both in Bodh Gaya and und the world; representatives m 12 countries now participate.

poche's centers have installed een 2½ ton World Peace Bells oly places, and have supported ovation projects at sacred sites, uding the historic renovation of Swayambhu Stupa in Nepal.

2005 Mangalam Light Founda- was established; operating ugh Ananda, Prajna, and Vajra ht Foundations, its mission is revive, preserve, and support

the heritage of the Buddha Dharma in Tibet. The Light Foundations have given substantial support to Tarthang Monastery, Larun Gar, Chokyab Gar, and Adzom Gar among other centers and over 1,000 sets of the Kanjur and 10,000 sets of the collected works of Kun khyen Longchenpa are being distributed to monasteries throughout Tibet.

In 2009, Rinpoche founded the Mangalam Research Center for Buddhist Languages in downtown Berkeley, followed by Dharma College and the Guna Foundation, a documentary film-making unit.

In 2013, he inaugurated Sarnath International Nyingma Institute to bridge the gap between East and West, support the study of the Khen Lob Cho Sum, and host the annual Tibet Peace Ceremony. The Nyingma Association of Mandala Organizations (NAMO) incorporated in 2012, helps guide and protect the work of its 17 member organizations.

Rinpoche has dedicated his life to preserve, protect, and distribute the Tibetan Buddhist heritage and manifest the sacred forms of kaya, vaca, citta, guna, and karma for the sake of the entire world. We cannot express all of his efforts here, but more information on the mandala's activities is recorded in the 45 volumes of the TNMC Annals.

Sarvam Mangalam
October 1, 2016